GALLANT SHIP, BRAVE MEN

Liberty Ship photo courtesy Imperial War Museum.

This book was printed in the United States of America.

To order additional copies of this book, contact:
Xlibris Corporation
1-888-795-4274
www.Xlibris.com
Orders@Xlibris.com
19023

COVER ILLUSTRATION

Lifeboat, painted by Lt. Griffith Foxley, USMS, in 1943, formerly was hung in Wiley Hall at the United States Merchant Marine Academy. More recently, however, the painting was moved and is now on display at the American Merchant Marine Museum at Kings Point, Long Island, New York.

Published By:

THE AMERICAN MERCHANT MARINE MUSEUM

THE UNITED STATES MERCHANT MARINE ACADEMY

GALLANT SHIP, BRAVE MEN

*The Heroic Story
of a WWII Liberty Ship*

Herman E. Rosen

CONTENTS

For my loving family:

Susan, my guiding star, who persevered and encouraged me;
Dan, Nancie, and Justice; Fred, Marge and Zoe

And

The Cadet-Midshipmen of the U.S. Merchant Marine Academy,
who, with courage and dedication, in war and peace,
go down to the sea in ships.

ACKNOWLEDGMENTS

I am indebted to:
Jim Hoffman, KP '44
The late Ronald B. Mackenzie, MD., KP '45 author of "Voyage of Destiny" (unpublished)
Captain Arthur B. Moore, KP '45 author of "A Careless Word . . . A Needless Sinking"
Robert Morris, O.S. aboard the John Drayton
Captain Charles M. Renick, KP, '47
"World War II, Day by Day," Longman Group and Chronicle Com. Ltd.
And especially to
The late Captain Carl Norman, my friend and mentor, without whose personal log, this account of the S/S John Drayton could not have been written
And finally,
Ileen Chopak and Ryan Panchadsaram, who diligently and patiently typed the manuscript.

INTRODUCTION

An integral part of the training at the United States Merchant Marine Academy at Kings Point, NY is the "Sea Year." Students spend a year, not on a training ship, but on regular operating merchant vessels. During times of war, they often found themselves in peril as they sailed through enemy-controlled water or unloaded military supplies in combat areas overseas. This was especially true during World War II when 142 Cadet-Midshipmen never returned to their home ports.

More than 600 other Cadet-Midshipmen were forced to abandon ship, sometimes more than once, when their vessels were sunk. Each of these men was required to submit a classified, detailed report of the enemy action that resulted in the sinking. In 1967, I discovered and rescued a file cabinet full of these "enemy action reports" that were about to be destroyed by an over-zealous "efficiency expert."

Reading these reports, written mostly by young men still in their teens, is both a sobering and inspiring experience. One report that especially stands out was written by Cadet-Midshipman Herman "Hank" Rosen about his 1942-43 voyage aboard the Liberty ship JOHN DRAYTON. The well written report is longer than most and tells a dramatic story of endurance and sacrifice of heroic proportions. Thirty days adrift in an open lifeboat without food or water is one of the epic tales to emerge from World War II.

Rosen's chronicle of the JOHN DRAYTON's voyage, which covered more than 17,000 miles and three oceans, is one of the best accounts I've seen anywhere about day-to-day life aboard a Liberty ship during the Second World War. The story will make fascinating reading to all those who love the sea, and especially to those who sailed during World War II and to all Kings Pointers, past, present, and future.

Capt. Charles M. Renick, USMS, USNR (Ret.)

Liberty ship under way. Winter, North Atlantic

CHAPTER I

Ship and Crew

My name is Herman Rosen, known as Hank, some call me Hy. I am 83 years old and like the other "Ancient Mariner," I have a story about a ship and her crew that must be told.

1940-41. There was war in Europe. German armies were mauling the British and the French. There was great pressure to bring the U.S. into the struggle on the side of the Allies.

Strong anti-war feeling was extensive in this country. I was a student at the University of Missouri, School of Journalism. The campus was roiled with protests against the war. Isolationist senators and professors spoke to groups on campus. Students gathered, marched and shouted, "Hell no! We won't go!"

A required course at the University was ROTC and our unit was Field Artillery. I hated the course. We had to drag around old World War I French 75 mm guns, while wearing heavy woolen uniforms, in 100 degree heat. Instruction was poor, the guns antiquated and the students made a joke of the course.

A regular army sergeant was our instructor and one day while we were "horsing around," he blew his whistle, pointed at us,

"Listen up, you guys," he said. "The United States is going to war soon. What you're learning here could one day save your life. Pay attention!" We did not take him seriously.

Then came December 7, 1941, the Japanese attack on Pearl Harbor. Anti-war sentiment changed overnight. Army and Navy recruitment offices were overwhelmed. Many students left school to enlist. I was concerned about being drafted into the army and assigned to Field Artillery because of previous ROTC training.

As a kid, I had always wanted to go to sea. I had read books like "Two Years Before the Mast," "Moby Dick," Mutiny on the Bounty," and Howard Pease's "The Tattooed Man." I was imbued with the romance of the sea, the sound of ship's bells and the smell of salt air.

An ad in a magazine caught my attention. There was a photograph of a young man in a midshipman's uniform. Beneath it read, "America's new ships have the finest officers afloat. Anxious to get in and pitch for America? Here's a way to serve your country now . . . . and have an opportunity for a fine future in peace time. Apply to the United States Merchant Marine Academy, today."

I left school soon after December 7 and started the application process for Kings Point. The Merchant Marine Academy at Kings Point, Long Island, New York is one of the five federal academies. The others are the Military, Naval, Coast Guard and Air Force.

In order to apply to Kings Point, a candidate must secure a letter of nomination from a member of Congress, pass an examination in English, math and science and pass a rigid physical, dental and eye exam. Candidates must be of good moral character, between 17 and 22 years of age, and never been married.

I passed the requirements, and in March, 1942, I was sworn in as Cadet, United States Merchant Marine Academy Cadet Corps, Midshipman U.S. Naval Reserve, and reported to the academy at Kings Point.

During the war the normal four year course at Kings Point was accelerated to 18 months. Students were required to spend three months at the academy in preliminary training, learning signaling, Morse code, seamanship, small boat handling, lifeboat skills, physical fitness, naval customs and traditions, radio, navigation and meteorology.

After three months as a plebe or 4th classman, the cadet shipped out for a minimum of six months at sea, where, deck cadets, under the tutelage of the captain and mates, and engine cadets, directed by the chief engineer and assistant engineers, learn their respective duties. While at sea, the cadet is a 3rd Classman.

During his six months at sea, in addition to shipboard duties, the cadet had an academy assignment, called the "Sea Project." This was a huge volume of required reading, math examinations, and written essays to be completed, and brought back to the academy for grading.

After sea duty and the approval of his Sea Project, the cadet returned to the academy for nine months of intensive training, the first three months as a 2nd Classman, and the final six months as a member of the 1st Class.

During his last six months, the cadet pursued a rigorous course of study in preparation for final exams, and license examinations given by the U.S. Coast Guard.

On graduation, cadets received a United States Merchant Marine Academy diploma, a license as 3rd Mate or 3rd Assistant Engineer on U.S. Merchant vessels, and a commission as Ensign in the U.S. Naval Reserve.

When my three month course at the academy was over, I was ordered with engine Cadet Tom Kellegrew to report to academy offices, downtown, New York. There, we met two other cadets who were joining us on the S/S John Drayton.

Cadets Peterson, deck, and Gabrielli, engine, pretended to be real "old salts." They had almost completed their assigned six months at sea, but needed only several more weeks, before returning to the academy for advanced training. They were assigned to the John Drayton to bring the ship to New York, when they would be taken off and replaced.

We four cadets journeyed together by rail to Wilmington, North Carolina, where the John Drayton, a Liberty ship, still on the ways, was being prepared for sea.

It was September, 1942 and the North Carolina countryside broiled in the heat. Riggers, welders, and riveters were clambering on board, rushing last minute details to launch the ship by September 17.

The cadets were permitted on board. We were able to inspect the ship, learn its details and get ready for launching. We found our quarters, on the port side in the midship house, near the radio shack. The room was small with little space between the upper and lower bunks, and the opposite bulkhead with a single porthole had a sink and a mirror.

On Thursday, September 17, according to plan, the crew came aboard and the ship was launched ready to sail. It was unknown to us at the time that a bloody battle had been fought in the North Atlantic only three days earlier. A wolfpack of 13 U-boats had stalked and harried convoy ON-127 for four days, sinking 12 freighters and one Canadian destroyer.

The John Drayton looked sleek and beautiful. She was 441 feet long, with a breadth of 56 feet and a draft of 27-1/2 feet. I counted the crew, totaling 56 men, as they came aboard, 41 merchant marine and 15 navy armed guard, led by Lt. Colwin.

The merchant crew was made up of deck and engine personnel and assigned watches 4 to 8, 8 to 12, and 12 to 4. There were a captain and three mates; chief mate, 2nd and 3rd mates; as well as chief engineer, 1st assistant, 2nd and 3rd assistant engineers. Then, the steward department made up of the chief steward, plus a number of cooks, bakers and messmen.

During the war, the United States was known as the "arsenal of democracy." Shipyards were building ships faster than one a day, and as a result, there was a huge need for crews.

Kings Point was graduating officers, while Sheepshead Bay was turning out ordinary seamen. Radio operators were being trained at schools throughout the country. "Upgrade"schools operated in several seaboard states where merchant seamen, who had put in the required length of time as able bodied seamen, could "sit" for license examinations as 3rd mate.

The need for crews was so great that many came aboard the

John Drayton and other ships, as ordinary seamen with no experience, their first time aboard a ship.

I was surprised at the difference in age between the youngsters and the "old salts" who had been to sea years ago in sailing vessels. Some of the crew were in their 60's, and others were 17 and 18 years old.

The cadets were introduced to the captain and the mates. The captain was cordial but businesslike. He had papers to sign, inspections to make, and he did not spend much time with us.

The mates were pleasant and interested in our studies. The chief mate, Oliver Westover, from Massachusetts, was a seasoned sailor, medium height and slim, in his mid-forties.

The 2nd mate, Mr. Kemp, was choleric and ruddy faced. He proudly wore his lieutenant commander uniform, but he struck me as being a roustabout.

Mr. Pruitt, the 3rd mate, from Maryland, was an older man, about sixty-five, who had not been to sea in years. He could have been a fisherman or a coastwise sailor. He did not seem to know very much about navigation or deep sea sailing.

On Friday, September 18, a fire and boat drill was held aboard the John Drayton. The shipyard workers completed work on the vessel. The steering gear, whistle, telegraph and engines were tested and found in good order and we departed for New York.

For the next four days, the John Drayton, riding high in the water, rolled, pitched and pounded. Confused seas and long swells made shambles of the galley. Dishes smashed to the deck, while messmen scrambled after pots and pans. Canned goods, not secured, slammed into bulkheads, swinging in rhythm from port to starboard.

One night, during our passage an AB, Van Buren Ethridge, reported sick. Medical attention was given to him, but he was unable to stand watch. The following morning, Ethridge was last seen at about 4:30 in the gunnery quarters, and about 5:00 he was reported missing.

The ship was searched from stem to stern, but Ethridge was not found. It was presumed that he was lost overboard, and it was so noted in the ship's log.

There was a good deal of grumbling on board after Ethridge disappeared. Some seamen said the ship was jinxed. It was not an auspicious beginning.

We proceeded up Chesapeake Bay toward the degaussing range. Degaussing was a process where the ship's hull was demagnetized, so that it did not set off devices in enemy magnetic mines, causing them to explode. The compass was adjusted to compensate for the demagnetization of the ship.

We arrived New York on Tuesday, September 29, and were taken by tug to Brooklyn pier #32 to load cargo. Cadets Peterson and Gabrielli were reassigned to the academy. They had completed their sea time. Cadets Morton Deitz, deck, and Jack Stadstad, engine, were assigned to the John Drayton in their stead. Tom Kellegrew and I remained on board.

In September, 1942, the battle for Stalingrad was at its height. German troops had penetrated the city's western and northern suburbs and Russian troops were counter attacking.

Soviet Marshall Zhukov was conscripting the civilian population to dig tank traps, while old men and young boys were preparing to defend the city. There was an urgent need for American war supplies and materiel.

After 12 days, the John Drayton was loaded to capacity. Nine Douglas A-20 bombers in crates and 14 Sherman tanks were dogged down on the deck. TNT and ammunition were loaded in #1 and #5 holds, while we flew the Baker flag. Mail marked "Bandar Shapour" and "Iran" was stowed aboard, along with airplane flares, jeeps, miscellaneous supplies, canned goods, boots, rainwear, machine tools and parts, small arms and a tremendous assortment of sacks of flour, food and materiel to feed and provision an army. The capacity of the ship was amazing. An untold number of slings were loaded on the dock, winched aboard, and lowered into the holds.

The Italian longshoremen were experienced and worked smoothly together, in gangs, on the dock and in the holds. The stowage was watched carefully by the chief mate, Mr. Westover, who had me standing by.

While loading the ship, I had occasion to be disciplined by the captain, and I feared that our relationship was off to a bad start. One day, I was taking pictures with my camera of the planes and the tanks on deck, and the slings that were going down into the hold. I heard a shout from the bridge, "Rosen . . . what in the hell are you doing? Come up here!" I went to the bridge and the captain said, "Give me that camera and I'll take care of it."

I feared that was a bad start for me, but apparently it didn't upset Captain Norman. He never mentioned it again.

Knowing that I lived in New York, the mate gave me permission to leave the ship evenings. I usually went home, riding the subway from Brooklyn to the Bronx, and trying hard to look like a salty old sea dog among the strap hanging land-lubbers.

We left New York on Sunday, October 11, 1942 and joined a convoy of 23 ships and five escorting destroyers. The ships flew flags of the Netherlands, Great Britain, Canada, and the U.S.

There were rumors aboard regarding our final destination. All hands agreed the cargo was destined for the Soviet Union. The tanks and crated planes were plainly stenciled in Russian, but the crew was concerned that we were heading for Murmansk.

Our position in the convoy was #53, meaning line five, third ship. Leading the convoy, eight ships across and three deep, was the commodore, position #51.

For the next several days we enjoyed good weather. The seas were calm and we proceeded southerly at about 8 knots. Life aboard the John Drayton settled down to routine. Deitz recovered from his miserable sea-sickness and the mate assigned us each lookout watch, from 8 p.m. to midnight, and midnight to 4:00 a.m.

Our job as lookout was to check the ship for complete blackout, draw the blackout curtains at dusk, and see that not a pinpoint of light shone anywhere about the ship. Then, to peer into the darkness for four hours, constantly searching for submarines.

Night watch for the mate was a difficult assignment. Traveling in convoy, he had to maintain station behind the ship directly ahead, and stay abreast of ships port and starboard.

In rough weather, the ships lumbered like elephants, as they pitched and rolled. The mate constantly ordered the helmsman, "Right a bit," or "left a bit." He often called the engine room to adjust engine revolutions.

Course changes at night always caused some anxiety. During the day, the commodore would signal a course change by flags, for example, "At 0100 change course to 150 degrees."

Each ship then acknowledged receipt of the signal by flying the same flags. The alert signalman had his flags two-blocked, almost as quickly as the commodore ship.

Then at 0100, out of the black void, a faint light blinked on the stern of the commodore ship, signaling the immediate course change to 150 degrees. The mate on watch would desperately hope that the ships around him were also swinging to 150 degrees.

One night, after I finished my watch 8 to 12, I had just climbed into my bunk, when the captain pounded on the door. "Hurry," he said, "Get to the panel board, the floodlights are on!"

I ran to the mainmast panel board on deck, where the floodlight switches were located. Our ship was lit up like a Christmas tree. Big glaring lights on the mainmast made daylight of the deck. The convoy about us had started to scatter.

The floodlights went off, just as I got to the panel. An engineer below had thrown the main switch.

The entire incident took about two minutes, yet many of the crew were already on deck, wearing life jackets and standing at lifeboat falls.

Tension lessened when a messman admitted flipping the wrong switch while trying to light up the galley. But some crew members muttered "jinxed ship."

We continued proceeding southerly in convoy. Much relieved, the cadets getting together, decided that we were not bound after all, for Murmansk. To us, the southerly route meant we were delivering the goods to the Russians via the Persian Gulf and Iran.

Deck cadet, Morton Deitz was tall, dark, usually quiet, a graduate of the University of Pennsylvania/Wharton School. He was about 22 years old from Trenton, New Jersey, a fine student. Somewhat religious, he read the Bible every day.

Mort was concerned about his thinning hair and asked the radio operator to clip him bald so that his hair would grow in stronger. Mort and I shared the same quarters, two in a room, upper and lower bunks. He was upper.

Engine cadet, Tom Kellegrew became my close friend. He worked hard at becoming an engineer. A high school graduate from Brooklyn, New York, tall, blue-eyed, with a genial disposition. Tom wanted to make a career of the sea. The Engine cadets also bunked together, two in a room.

Engine cadet, Jack Stadstad was about 20 years old, handsome, about 6 ft. tall, blond, blue-eyed, with a light fuzz of a beard. He had some college. He was relaxed and easy-going, from Garden City, Long Island. Jack brought aboard a hand-wind phonograph with only one record, "White Christmas," by Bing Crosby, that he played, over and over again.

The radio operator Niel Nielson, we called "Sparks," was from Florida. He was a pleasant fellow who had polio as a child, and as a result, wore a heavy brace on one leg. Sparks was short, and his upper body was strong. He could easily chin 30 to 40 times. The radio room, called the "shack," was next to ours, midship, and Sparks slept near his radio.

We also carried the ship's purser, Mr. Daly, who was responsible for the ship's finances. In port, you saw the purser for a draw against your pay, money to spend ashore. Mr. Daly was married, a soft-spoken, educated gentleman from New Rochelle, New York, "who liked to lift a glass."

The Navy armed guard of 15 men was responsible for manning the 5" gun on the stern, the 3" gun forward and, with the cadets, the four 20 mm anti-aircraft guns midship.

The navy men also stood regular lookout watches with the merchant marine crew. They were quartered near the stern, and ate with the merchant crew. Led by a petty officer, the coxswain, the armed guard reported to Lt. Colwin.

A sturdy fellow from Texas, Lt. Colwin had a good working

relationship with Captain Norman, the merchant marine officers and cadets. He ate with us in the officers' mess. Well trained, always affable, Lt. Colwin had the respect of all on board.

CHAPTER II

Guantanamo Bay

On Sunday, October 18, 1942 our convoy arrived in Guantanamo Bay, Cuba, after an uneventful seven days at sea. We had traveled 1355 miles at an average speed of 8.82 knots. Several ships in the convoy continued southerly, while we dropped anchor in 30 fathoms in the bay. There was to be no shore leave, and scuttlebutt had it that we would be here for about two days.

As we were going through the submarine protection nets at Guantanamo, it occurred to me that most of the American public was still unaware of the deadly submarine warfare going on just off the East Coast and in the Caribbean.

During the first six months of 1942, the unbelievable toll of U.S. merchant vessels torpedoed and sunk, was 231, of which a significant number went down off the east coast and in the Caribbean.

Tankers and merchant ships had been easy targets, silhouetted against the blazing lights of New York, Atlantic City and other coastal ports. It was only a few months ago that a complete blackout of coastal cities had been ordered.

The following morning, Monday, October 19, after anchoring in Guantanamo Bay, I was awakened by a loud explosion aboard the John Drayton. My first thought was we had struck a mine. All the lights were out and dense steam was coming up from the engine room.

The chief engineer was rushing from his room with a towel wrapped around his head. He shouted to me "Grab an emergency light and follow me down to the engine room!" Steam columns were so dense that my light was barely visible. We got to the boiler room and helped Mr. Harris, the 1st assistant engineer, up through a ventilator. He was grimy and shaken.

The chief and I ran to the engine room where he called out the names of engineers on watch. Suddenly, he spun around and said, "Oh my God, the old man is down there!" He was referring to Anton Hagerup, 3rd assistant engineer, about 70 years old.

Some navy gunners joined us as we got down to the engine room where the steam was dense but clearing. The 3rd assistant was lying face down on the landing near the main line, a rasping sound coming from his throat. Someone ran for a blanket, and while slipping and sliding in the muck, we managed a makeshift stretcher and got the old man to the deck.

Mr. Hagerup's left arm was completely severed below the elbow. His jugular vein was cut and his windpipe exposed. Blood was spurting from his neck. Deep cuts were also visible on other parts of his body. We kept applying pressure.

Lying out in the middle of the bay, we tried to call shoreside for a doctor. We hoisted the "William" flag, meaning "medical attention urgently needed." We used the blinker lights. We bent the ensign to the staff, upside down, used semaphore flags, and even fired 20 millimeter guns, but we roused no one. Mr. Hagerup died in about 20 minutes. He had never regained consciousness.

About a half hour later, Navy doctor, Sullivan, arrived in a launch, examined the body and left with it, to be placed in the morgue and attended to in accordance with naval procedure. A pall lay over the entire ship and remarks were heard again that the ship was jinxed. This was the second man lost, Ethridge over the side, and now, Anton Hagerup.

At about 2:50 p.m. navy chief petty officer Cook came aboard to assess the damage. He found the ship's three generators had completely disintegrated. He advised Captain Norman he would try to arrange auxiliary power for the ship's lights and refrigeration. Two hours later a navy repair barge secured alongside and connected power lines to the John Drayton. At 6:30 p.m. power was cut in.

The following morning, Tuesday, October 20, the shore station blinked "Anton Hagerup would be buried today at 2:00 p.m. His shipmates are asked to attend." Captain Norman, however, said the ship would be moved at 3:00 p.m. and the men on watch had to be on board. Finally, 13 of us could go, Mr. Hagen, 2nd assistant engineer, Sparks, three cadets in uniform and eight navy sailors in dress whites.

Mr. Hagerup was buried in a naval cemetery, atop a small hill in Cuba. Last rites were administered by navy Chaplain Lt. Harris in a brief service as we stood in a tight little circle around the grave.

Early next day, naval intelligence officer, Lt. Young and several officials and machinists came aboard to investigate the accident again, and to ascertain the damage, and the extent of repairs. Engine room damage was extensive. Two complete generators, a flywheel and governor, steam valves, engine valves, flanges, etc. had to be replaced or repaired.

In the meantime, the captain and the chief engineer were busy making trips from ship to shore, meeting with officials and advising New York of the damage and the urgent need for replacement parts.

There were many more days of delay. Naval officials came aboard almost daily, met with the captain and chief engineer, investigated again and again, but had no word for us regarding parts or repairs.

Days passed. Morale on board ship was low. Make work was found for us . . . . scraping, oiling, painting. Still no word . . . Finally to allay the boredom, the captain and Lt. Colwin were able to arrange for 21 men, eight armed guard and 13 merchant seamen, to go ashore and use the navy firing range.

We were up at dawn. The steward's department prepared a carton of sandwiches and apples, and after waiting several hours for transportation, we got to the range at last. We were given detailed instructions on the mechanism and use of our 20 millimeter anti-aircraft guns.

After lunch an aircraft towing a target sleeve flew over. Each man was given 80 rounds and on the third trip over, the target was destroyed. Our instructors were pleased with the results.

The naval base at Guantanamo, which sailors call "Gitmo," lies at the easternmost part of Cuba. It is a huge establishment and in addition to the firing range and airfield, there is a hospital, repair shop, movie house, canteen, PX, and quarters for hundreds of sailors. It is a virtual city, like a U.S. fiefdom in Cuba.

The base is strategically located at a point where the Atlantic ocean meets the Caribbean sea and it is positioned to defend approaches to the Panama Canal, as well as the southeastern coast of the United States.

The following day, a British ship the "Empire Waimana" moored near us and soon, we were shouting across and learned that two English cadets were aboard. We invited them to visit. They were amazed at our food, living quarters, and pay. We earned $65.00 a month. They got 10 pounds. Their uniforms and training were similar to ours. Their food was poor, but they were issued two bottles of beer each day. We swapped magazines and souvenirs and they invited us to visit them the next day.

Their ship, a thirty-one year old coal burner, 122 man crew, made 8.5 knots, and carried refrigerated cargo to England from New Zealand. It was presently on a return trip to New Zealand with general cargo. The cadets told us about Malta convoys, life in England and of the thousands of American troops training there.

The next night we returned the visit. We played darts, drank New Zealand beer, met their officers, and gave the cadets matches, soap, toothpaste, and fruit. It was greatly appreciated.

The Empire Waimana pulled out the following morning. We

hoisted the flags "PYU" meaning "good voyage" and they returned, "thanks." A cadet was at the halyard. We were sorry to see them go.

At about 2:00 p.m. there was an air raid alert. Sparks woke me and I went to my gun station and waited in the glaring sun for over an hour and a half, for something to happen. At 3:40 p.m., the navy signal tower hauled down the Baker flag signifying "all clear."

I worked all day with Chips, the ship's carpenter, and the chief mate, looking for our ship's tools which were strewn all over the deck. We finally found them all and stowed them in the ship's locker.

The shore station gave us news of the war, which continued to sadden and frustrate us. Here we were tied up in Guantanamo Bay with cargo of planes, tanks and ammunition destined for Russia, while the Soviet armies were reeling at Stalingrad. Yet, there seemed to be little effort ashore to complete our repairs and get us underway.

Sunday, November 1, Captain Norman gave us permission to use the #4 lifeboat. Mr. Brainovich, the chief engineer, Mr. Kemp, 2nd mate, Tom Kellegew, five sailors and I, lowered the boat and set sail. Not much of a breeze, but we got around and sailed for about two hours, looking over the other ships in the bay. We discovered cadets from New Orleans aboard the "Curacao." We came back at about 3:30 p.m. using sails and oars.

This evening, a new 3rd assistant engineer, Mr. Hood, reported aboard. He seemed like a fine fellow, about 32 years old. He flew from New York to Miami, then to Havana, and finally Guantanamo. All told, it took him two days.

The next day, another air raid alert. All guns were manned, but no hostile aircraft appeared. Many planes took off from the Gitmo airfield. I had been assigned to the 20 mm gun on the port side of the bridge with AB's Soderberg and Hudgins. Later I spent most of the day greasing davits with an alemite gun. Davits are a type of crane that hang over the side of the ship, used in lowering lifeboats.

We had fire and boat drill about once a week, when all hoses were led out on deck. Lifeboats were swung out, ready for launching. They were then checked to be sure they were provisioned and the fresh water changed. The water was carried in a 20 gallon keg.

On Tuesday, November 3, a large convoy arrived and a Liberty ship, "William Patterson" blinked to us that she had some information for the master. At 11:00 a.m. the following day, a towboat and barge came alongside with our generator parts from the Patterson. There was real excitement on board.

The chief engineer, however, discovered that one important piece of machinery was missing. We signaled the Patterson, and they replied that all the parts had had been sent over.

Again the chief and the captain were bitter at the inefficiency existing all along the line. No one seemed to give a damn about us. Each man passed the buck. With millions of dollars worth of vital cargo, planes, and tanks on board, one would think that more concern would be shown.

The chief would not even venture a guess as to how long we'd be here. He said he would try to get the navy to weld the pieces together, but he was not optimistic.

Friday, November 6, the navy had been working on our generators for the past two days, and up to the present, not much seemed to have been accomplished. Parts were still strewn all over the deck.

The daily schedule was, navy boat arrives at 9:30 a.m. The men, about six, sit around and talk until about 10:00. Then they turn to for about an hour. They adjourn for coffee at 11:00, and turn to for another half hour, before knocking off for lunch. And so on for the balance of the day. When they leave about 4:00 p.m., little or nothing has been accomplished. Captain Norman seemed powerless. He went ashore each day, but nothing came of it.

We cadets used our free time to work on our sea projects and to familiarize ourselves with the ship. We learned more about each other and the ship's officers, both deck and engine.

Tom Kellegrew, engine cadet, and I became fast friends. He was a dedicated engineer and I noted that the chief took a special interest in him. It was similar for me, in that Captain Norman often approved of my work on board.

The skipper and I laughed about one project in particular. He told me one day to paint, white, the ventilator caps on the bridge. These look like mushroom caps. They are about one foot in diameter and open to about one foot above the deck. The caps are opened or closed by turning them on a screw shaft. Their purpose is to bring air down to the chart room and to the sleeping quarters below.

In the dark, when the ship is blacked out, the ventilator caps can be a hazard, therefore, the white paint. In painting the caps, I simply held the brush, loaded with paint, in the middle of the cap, then spun the cap around, so that it actually painted itself in a very neat circle with no drips.

The captain watched and said, "That's a great idea. You ought to patent it and we'll sell it to other ships. Well done."

There was no spit and polish authority between the captain, the mates and cadets, but an easy relationship existed. We cadets, however, were respectful, and the deck officers and engineers were pleased to help us.

Sparks, the ship's radio officer, also became a good friend. He regaled us with stories of the trips he made at sea and, despite the handicap of his heavy brace, he was in constant good spirits.

To some people, things seemed to come easily. Engine Cadet Jack Stadstad was just such a fellow. While Tom Kellegrew, worked hard, Jack did things easily and naturally. He had a fine working relationship with the officers and crew. He was well-liked and, of course, played his favorite and only record, "White Christmas."

Morton Dietz, my fellow deck cadet, was a good student and a quick learner. Despite being woefully seasick for several days after leaving New York, he gamely tried to stand his watches. In Guantanamo, in better spirits, Mort worked diligently on his sea project.

For some fun and entertainment, the mates and Lt. Colwin tried to arrange a lifeboat race between the merchant marine crew and the navy gun crew. Plans were set and there was excitement on board, but the race had to be called off because of traffic in the bay. However, at dinner, the chief engineer told us that at last, work was progressing on the generators and, he hoped, we would be leaving in the near future. This was after four weeks at anchor, or moored, in the bay.

Thursday, November 12 was Armistice Day. Here at Guantanamo there was no special activity. The navy machinists were working on our generators below.

At about 7:15 p.m. there was another air raid alert. In less than two minutes, all our guns were manned ready for action. There was a complete blackout in the bay, but no enemy aircraft was sighted. Everyone was of the opinion that enemy planes could come from Martinique. The alert lasted about 50 minutes.

The following day, I worked with Charlie Kardos, an AB, most of the afternoon straightening out the lamp locker.

Saturday, November 14, was a pleasant day. We went ashore, Deitz, the 3rd assistant engineer, Lt. Colwin, and several of the navy gun crew, expecting to go to the firing range. We were told, however, that the range was closed. We persuaded the Lieutenant to remain ashore for a short while to do some shopping. We visited the ship's store, where everything in the line of food could be purchased.

Lt. Colwin invited the cadets to lunch in the officer's mess, where we enjoyed steak and potatoes, cookies and dessert. A navy lieutenant commander gave us a lift back to the pier and a small boat brought us back to the ship, but we were soaked to the skin from the spray. Ashore, I heard that we would be leaving Guantanamo within a couple of days.

We learned of the successful Allied landing in North Africa, despite French resistance. According to reports, French defenders fired on American troops, pinning them down in Casablanca. It was only after suffering heavy casualties that the Allies were able to take the beaches.

The surprise to us was the fierce fight put up by the French navy. Several British and American ships were sunk, or damaged, with considerable losses of troops and naval personnel, before the Vichy forces were defeated.

The weather in Guantanamo turned hot. The air was completely still. Ashore, the trees looked dusty and tired. We took to sleeping on deck. It was cooler in the open and the nights under the stars were unforgettable.

Sunday, November 15. Today marked the beginning of our fifth week in Guantanamo, but also, our last day here. After conferences ashore, yesterday and this afternoon, the skipper said we would be leaving tomorrow. In fact, he ordered me to hoist #33, our convoy number.

It was good news. All of us were anxious to be back on the high seas again. There was much speculation on board whether we were headed for Trinidad and the Caribbean, or Panama. With the increased number of sinkings around the northern coast of South America, it seemed more likely that we would go through the Panama Canal and down along the west coast of South America to avoid submarines.

In any event, the mate told me that we were still scheduled for Bandar Shapour in the Persian Gulf. He said not to expect to get back to the States before May.

There was almost a holiday atmosphere aboard. Everyone turned in early so that we could be up and ready in the morning. We were scheduled to leave at 7:35 a.m. the next day, after spending 28 days, 22 hours in Guantanamo. Sadly, we had buried our 3rd assistant in a Naval cemetery, and we were looking forward to a new beginning.

Despite the long and oppressive delay in the bay, there were some light moments and one involved Jack. Afternoons in the bay were hot. Temperatures exceeded 100 degrees and, occasionally, a cadet or a crew member, would slip over the side for a quick swim.

One afternoon, Jack came up after assisting in the engine room, hot and sweaty, and decided to go for a swim. An athlete and a fine swimmer, he was determined to "swan" dive from the stern of the ship. Some of the crew and armed guard shouted their encouragement as he stripped down to his shorts.

Jack climbed over the rail and started a graceful swan dive. About halfway down, he and everyone else saw a six foot shark moving slowly just about where Jack was to hit the water. The swan became a screaming, backpaddling, clawing cadet. He hit the water feet first with a tremendous splash. The startled shark and the fallen swan took off like jets in opposite directions. There was to be no more swimming from the deck of the John Drayton.

CHAPTER III

Panama Canal

U p at 6:00 a.m., navy tug alongside starboard quarter, at 6:45: . . . 7:33 . . . let go lines fore and aft . . . 8:24 a.m . . . Departure. Outside the submarine nets, we picked up the convoy, 17 ships, including a troop transport, 11 escorting vessels and several planes overhead. Judging from the direction of the compass, we were heading for Panama.

Heavy swells all morning and cadet Deitz seasick again. Several of the gun crew were also leaning over the rail, a sure sign that we were back at sea.

We had a fire and boat drill at 2:30 p.m. and an air raid drill at about 4:00 p.m. Guns were manned in two minutes. At 9:30 p.m. escorting vessels on the starboard quarter let go two depth charges and for the balance of the night everyone held his lifejacket.

At 12:00 midnight Deitz called me and I stood a four hour watch with Mr. Kemp, the 2nd mate. It was a beautiful moonlit night. We passed Morant Point at 12:15 a.m., traveling at good speed with close convoy protection.

The next day we had a following sea, still making excellent

time. The chief mate helped me use the stadometer and I computed 1675 feet between us and the convoy commodore. I took a turn at the wheel for about an hour and held the commodore on the port bow.

While standing the 4:00 to 8:00 a.m. watch with Mr. Westover, he pointed out various constellations. We could see clearly Orion and the stars Betelgeuse, Bellatrix, Rigel and Sirius. The stars were readily identifiable and the mate said he often used them for navigation.

The convoy speed was about 11 knots, adjusted to accommodate the slower Libertys. There were no coal burners, or antiquated Hog Islanders, to act as a drag. The mate said, at this rate, and, if the weather holds up, we should get into Panama, Thursday, November 19. There were no stragglers, and the moonlit nights allowed for good station keeping.

The Troop Transport, which undoubtedly could move faster than 11 knots, was well protected in the middle of the convoy. The escort vessels, corvettes and sub chasers, raced back and forth, kicking up lots of foam. There was still plenty of air protection.

The next day, I was on 4:00 to 8:00 a.m. watch with the mate again, in pouring rain. We were in sight of land as the watch ended, and arrived Panama Canal Zone 12:15 p.m., Thursday, November 19, as the mate anticipated.

We stopped first at Quarantine anchor and then moved to the dock for fuel and water. All hands were expecting to go ashore in the morning.

Friday, November 20 at about 10:00 a.m., Tom and I went ashore in Cristobal, Panama, with the navy gun crew and Lt. Colwin. After getting across the slip, we left the gun crew and hailed a ride to town. We shopped a bit and went to the officers' club in Colon for lunch.

The towns of Colon and Cristobal were separated by railroad tracks. Both were carnival towns where the main industry was confined to the brothels. There were many ladies of various ages and hues intent on soliciting business. Each block had at least one dozen gin mills, nightclubs, and dives.

When Tom and I headed back to the dock, a little black kitten, meowing and looking for a handout, rubbed against my leg. When we got back on board, I had the cat tucked under my arm.

Sparks was delighted and immediately named the kitten, "Inky." He rushed down to the galley and came back with a saucer of milk, cementing Inky's friendship.

It was love at first sight. Inky made her home in the shack while Sparks was on duty, and when Sparks went to his room, the kitten followed at his heels.

Back on board Tom and I were sorry to learn that Mr. Hagen, the 2nd assistant engineer, was ill and taken to the hospital. He was Tom's favorite engineer and popular on board the John Drayton. He played the guitar, sang folk songs and kept us, and the crew, entertained. The chief said he would have to wire New York for Hagen's replacement.

However, during the night, the port captain advised that a 1st assistant engineer, John Wainio, was looking for a berth. Captain Norman signed him on, and Mr. Wainio agreed to serve as 2nd assistant on the John Drayton.

On Saturday, November 21 we entered the Panama Canal. Twelve marines and six sailors all well armed accompanied us. It took approximately 8 hours to go through the Gatun locks, #1, #2, #3, the lake, Peter McGill lock and finally, Mira Flores locks #1 and #2 made up the canal. I stood by the engine telegraph ringing up commands of the pilot throughout the entire trip.

We arrived Balboa shortly after 9:00 p.m. and loaded 10,000 barrels of oil, 500 tons of fresh water, in addition to food, before heading out to sea.

Some of the crew had gone to the captain to object to Inky, to having a black cat aboard. Captain Norman listened attentively and finally agreed. Inky had to go.

The marines accompanying us through the canal, took the cat ashore in Balboa. Sparks was heartbroken, but we told him Inky made history. She was, no doubt, the only cat in the world, who hitchhiked from Colon to Balboa, through the Panama Canal. We convinced Sparks that the marines had adopted Inky and gave her a good home.

While in Balboa, we learned more of the war's progress. In North Africa over 4,000 men died in the battle between Allied invasion forces and local French troops. In Oran, 17 French warships were sunk and the entire French fleet at Casablanca was destroyed.

News from Stalingrad, too, was encouraging. The Russians were holding on despite constant battering. German infantry was forced to fight house to house, door to door, by stubborn Russian defenders.

We admired the Russians who were counter-attacking, in spite of being outmanned and outgunned. We hoped they could hold out until Allied munitions and supplies poured in.

CHAPTER IV

Around the Horn

Our final destination and route now was no longer in doubt. We were heading for the Persian Gulf, and to avoid submarines, we were routed down the west coast of South America, around Cape Horn, the southernmost tip of South America, across the south Atlantic to Capetown, South Africa. Our course along the coast was 193 deg., 212 and 214. It was expected we would be at sea 40 days before the next port.

The captain ordered all lifeboats swung out and kept in readiness. All members of the crew and armed guard were warned to keep a complete blackout at night, a real sharp lookout, and to be ready for an attack at all times.

The mate arranged for Deitz and me to work with the bo'sun every morning, and spend the afternoon studying. In addition, during his watch, 4 to 8, he asked me to take turns at the wheel.

We were experiencing moderate to fresh southerly winds and rough seas. Despite the heavy seas, the captain told the chief engineer, he would like to make 10½ knots, if possible, in order for the navy to know our approximate position at all times.

On Tuesday, November 24, battle stations were manned. Two empty oil drums were tossed over the side and all guns began firing, 5" forward, 3" aft, and 20 mm guns midships. Both targets were hit eventually. The captain and Lt. Colwin expressed satisfaction in our marksmanship.

The skipper, then, asked the chief engineer to increase speed to 64 revolutions per minute. At 5:50 p.m. we passed the Equator from north to south.

Working with the bo'sun, I got the opportunity to know him. He was a man in his late fifties, of Scandinavian stock. He had been to sea for many years, starting back in sailing ships. Tattooed on four fingers of each hand were the letters HOLD FAST. I assumed it was descriptive of hanging on to lines and rigging on sailing ships.

The bo'sun was half drunk all the time. He was supposed to be the leader of the deck gang, but I noticed they did not have much regard for him. Two experienced ABs, Soderberg and Tobiassen, were kind to the old man and, without brushing him aside, took over leadership of the deck gang.

The mate was aware of the shortcomings of the bo'sun and, although he directed his orders to the old man, he looked to Ed Soderberg and Nick Tobiassen to carry them out.

The bo'sun kept us busy, checking the stays on the deck cargo, checking the gear and equipment, painting and oiling.

We were proceeding southerly, light swells, with gentle to light breeze when the captain called me to the bridge and said, he wanted me to start painting the top of the main mast. A bo'sun chair was rigged. I was given a brush, a bucket of gray paint on a line was secured to the side of the chair.

In a few moments I was hoisted to the top of the mast about 60 feet above the deck and, as the ship rolled, I swung out from port to starboard, trying frantically to get a few strokes of paint on the mast, while hanging on for dear life.

After a while, the captain blew a whistle and told the AB to bring me down. He said, "Rosen, well done. You'll make a good ship's officer. Next time put a line around the mast. It'll keep you from swinging out." I felt like I had passed a test.

We have been running alone in the Pacific, ever since leaving the Panama Canal. Not far off the west coast of South America, we passed Colombia, Ecuador, Peru, and we have not seen another ship.

Our mission, of course, was to get our cargo, safely, to the Persian Gulf and, eventually to Russia. Submarines were still wreaking havoc in the Atlantic. The more direct route for us to the Persian Gulf, would have been across the Atlantic to the Mediterranean, through the Suez Canal, but our cargo was too precious to risk the shorter, but more hazardous route.

Two of our crew, Billy Fontaine and Bob Morris were inseparable buddies. About 18 years old, they were ordinary seamen from Meridien, Mississippi who signed on the John Drayton to do their part in the war and to seek adventure at sea. Both had made one prior trip.

Billy, modestly told us of his trip to Murmansk when his convoy was decimated by German subs and aircraft. He was relieved that we were destined for the Persian Gulf.

Bob had been a messman aboard another ship. Both Billy and Bob were willing hands aboard the John Drayton.

Thursday, November 26, Thanksgiving, was a memorable day. The steward department went all out and prepared an outstanding dinner comprised of fruit cocktail, cream of tomato soup, roast turkey and dressing, baked ham in wine sauce, mashed potatoes, green peas, sliced cucumbers and finally, pumpkin pie. A great holiday spirit was on board.

Our messman, Hutchinson, a black man from the West Indies, was all smiles as he carried heaping platters to our table. We cadets ate together and he favored us with extra tidbits.

Hutchinson was an experienced messman, well spoken and apparently, well educated. A gray haired gentleman about fifty, who despite sloping decks and high seas, never spilled a drop.

Working with the captain, I noted our position at 6 deg., 52 min. south, latitude, and 83 deg., 35 min. west, longitude. We were making 10 knots, course 175 deg. The weather was partly cloudy. Temperature 70 degrees with light head winds.

The skipper pointed out our position on the chart. Peru was abeam. We were traveling due south. He noted we could take one of two courses. Either, go through the Straits of Magellan into the south Atlantic, or go around Cape Horn. He did not commit himself.

Days passed. The weather turned cloudy and the seas rough.

An engine room wiper Browning, reported sick to the chief engineer, who told him to see the captain. Captain Norman determined that Browning was suffering from a sinus attack. He said it was not serious and advised Browning to go back to work.

Captain Norman was a kindly man who had come up through the "hawse pipe," which in sailor's terms, means he had started at sea years ago as an ordinary seaman and worked his way up through the ranks.

The captain was married, no children, and he oftimes spoke fondly of his wife, Betty. He was blond, blue-eyed, about 5 ft. 8 in., muscular, with rugged features. An able navigator and seaman, he had the respect of his officers and crew.

Invariably, the skipper would start his breakfast with a raw egg, which he neatly punctured at each end, and then sucked out. I noticed, when the ship was rolling, Mr. Pruitt, the 3rd mate, always looked the other way.

The chief mate, Oliver Westover, was a slight, sensitive man, who sometimes recited poetry on watch. He certainly was not the burly, hard-as-nails mate, often portrayed in popular movies.

Mr. Westover was not a happy man. He constantly groused about the ship and its shortcomings. "It was too unwieldy, or it lumbered, and it labored, or it rode too high, or too low, and the seas washed over its deck."

The chief mate, often referred to on ships as "the mate," arranged for Deitz and me to rotate watches. We were to alternately stand watch with him, the 2nd, and the 3rd mate, so that they could get to know us, and teach us their respective duties.

Aboard ship, the chief mate acts as Executive Officer. He is in charge of the bo'sun and the deck gang. He is also in charge of overseeing the loading and discharging cargo. Only the captain can override his orders. The chief mate stands the 4 to 8 watch, 4:00 a.m., to 8:00 a.m., and 4:00 p.m. to 8:00 p.m.

The 2nd mate, who stands the 12:00 to 4:00 watch, is the navigating officer on board ship. He is in charge of fixing our position, moving the clocks on board and maintaining the ship's charts at all times. Our 2nd mate, Mr. Kemp, was a devil-may-care guy, lax in discipline, but apparently skilled at his craft.

The 3rd mate aboard the John Drayton was Mr. Pruitt, a family man. His duty, it seemed, was to maintain the 8:00 to 12:00 watch, and keep his station in convoy.

The captain, of course, was in overall charge. He seemed to be on the bridge, more often, than not. He did not run a tight ship, but he knew what was going on at all times.

In the engine room, Tommy and Jack had positions and learning experiences similar to ours. They stood regular watches with the engineers.

The chief engineer, Mr. Brainovich was in charge, 1st assistant engineer, Mr. Harris, 2nd assistant, Mr. Wainio, and 3rd assistant, Mr.Hood stood watches at times similar to the deck officers. They worked closely with the cadets and helped in their studies. Tom and Jack told us of what they were learning and seemed happy about conditions below.

Tuesday, December 1. The weather was cloudy. We were experiencing moderate to rough seas, heavy swells. The wind was southeast force 4-5.

Navy armed guard, Spellings, reported sick and the captain and Lt. Colwin tried to diagnose his illness. Apparently the man's condition became worse since leaving Guantanamo Bay, where he was examined by a doctor, who could not find anything radically wrong.

The doctor had prescribed salt tablets. Spelling still complained of severe pain in his legs and knees. He said, he eats normally, but has had no bowel movement for some time. He was very weak and complained of pain in the abdomen and also gas.

Captain Norman gave Spellings some bicarbonate of soda and about an hour later, Lt. Colwin gave him an enema. Spellings was taken off duty and removed to the ship's sick bay.

Sparks has been busy, sporadically, in the radio shack since we left the canal. He gave messages to the captain and was secretive about them. He never told us what he was sending or receiving.

A message came in today and Sparks hurried to the bridge to see the captain. Not long afterwards, the skipper called a fire and boat drill and cautioned the crew against panic if torpedoed. He told the men the greatest danger was in stampede. He pointed out lifeboats, life rafts, and life jackets are all precautionary measures, that if used properly, can save lives.

Captain Norman, then, directed the cadets to empty a lifeboat and display the equipment in the boat, hatchet, flares, cans of pemmican, water cask, first aid kit, etc.

The skipper impressed the crew with the importance of blackouts and ordered no light be shown from any porthole at night. Cadets, he said, would continue to be responsible for blackout security. One hour before sundown we were to tour the entire ship and draw blackout curtains. There was to be no smoking on deck after sundown.

The men secured the fire hoses, sobered by the captain's speech. The war seemed so far away that some thought the "old man" was too cautious. One said, "We've been in the Pacific almost two weeks and not even sighted another ship."

The captain was concerned about Spellings. He visited him in the sick bay and told Spellings he would give him all the care possible. He said Spellings was quite cheerful. The captain also instructed the steward department to prepare special meals for the sick armed guardsman.

Saturday, December 5, our position was 40 deg. 20 min. south latitude; longitude 81 deg. 10 min. west. Our course was 176 deg. and our speed slightly under 10 knots. We were in the "Roaring Forties." The seas were huge, breaking over the deck. A line was rigged up on deck so that we could "Hold Fast" while getting to our lookout posts.

Chile was abeam on the portside, but, we were too far offshore and could not see land. Winds were high, force 5 to 6. The Roaring Forties were aptly named.

The following morning, at 12:12 a.m., the auto alarm went off in the radio shack. Everyone at this point was a bit jumpy. We saw Sparks scurrying up to the captain's quarters. We made sure life jackets were readily available.

Later that day, after breakfast, the captain announced the S/S Harvey W. Scott, a Liberty ship, was experiencing a crack in the ship's side, and asked ships in the area to report their positions. The skipper said, the Scott was not in need of immediate assistance, and would try to proceed to the Straits of Magellan under her own steam. In the evening, he reported a new message. The Scott was making good time and expected to be at Punta Arenas at the Straits, in good order.

The John Drayton was rolling heavily now. The wind had increased to force 8, a moderate gale. We were ordered to make certain the lifeboats and rafts were firmly secured.

As we progressed further into southern latitudes, the days became longer. Nightfall one night was after 10:00 p.m. and daybreak the following morning was 2:00 a.m. The seas became rougher and we were taking them over the boat deck. Storm doors were dogged down.

Sleeping became a chore. It was impossible with the ship swinging like a pendulum, 25 deg. port, then upright, and then 25 deg. starboard. I tried to manage by propping pillows between my back and the bulkhead.

Temperature 51 deg., the barometer was falling steadily. The winds, now a fresh gale, shifted to the north/northwest. Heavy seas broke over the deck continually and the mate was concerned about the deck cargo.

Chips, the ship's carpenter, and a number of ABs checked the stays carefully making certain the Sherman tanks and crated planes were fully secured. Chips also checked the hatches and secured the tarpaulins. He was constantly tapping in new wedges around all hatches. All doors were dogged tight and men on board were warned again to be particularly careful. The high winds tore at the rigging. Anyone on deck was in danger of being swept overboard.

Three albatrosses were following the ship. Opinion among

the crew was equally divided. Some thought it was a good omen and others believed it was a sign of a jinxed ship. I fed the birds some bread and they circled until the bread was well astern before they settled on the water to eat. The lookout sighted some whales off the port bow. They were spouting and traveling in a pod about 2 miles off.

We took numerous azimuths and they indicated we had a compass error of 36 deg. easterly. It was a troublesome note. It meant we had to be particularly wary of our compass course and direction.

On deck we were dressed in rubber suits, covered from head to foot with only eyes and nose exposed. There was a cold wind chill, although the air temperature was 49 deg. and sea temperature, 45 deg. The barometer was holding steady at 29.66.

Thursday, December 10, after only four hours of darkness, we started passing around Cape Horn, from west to east. Numerous penguins were observed and many ice floes alongside. The three albatrosses continued following the ship. Our position was 56 deg. 40 min. south, 69 deg. 20 min. west, speed 9.4 knots.

I thought of the old wooden ships and iron men and how they battled their way along the same course, fighting wind and sea and ice.

At 6:30 p.m. we were at the 75th meridian. Cape Horn was bearing true north, 20 miles. The vessel was now in the Atlantic Ocean. On board, clocks were advanced one hour.

Later that evening, armed guardsman, Travelstead was found passed out, lying on deck outside his bunk. He was brought inboard and Lt. Colwin was advised. The lieutenant thought Travelstead was ill. In the sick bay, Spellings appeared to be improving.

There were 15 armed guard aboard the John Drayton, including Lt. Colwin. The chain of command was the lieutenant to the coxswain, a petty officer, who was in charge of the squad. Included in the navy detail were two signalmen.

The coxswain was a slight, fair haired country boy, who was recently married. He shyly showed us a wedding photo. The navy men, some were really boys, seventeen and eighteen years old, were dominated by Travelstead, a big, strong fellow, a pig farmer from Missouri. Travelstead openly showed his disdain for the coxswain.

After passing into the South Atlantic, we, at last, experienced fair weather, alto-cumulus clouds and long, low southwesterly swells. But the barometer remained low and steady.

Travelstead was kept in bed and Spellings was up to shave and shower. He had a normal bowel movement the first in two weeks.

The albatrosses continued to follow the ship. They were white bodied with gray on top of their wings. We often saw penguins, whales, and sea lions.

Monday, December 14, during the night we advanced the clocks one hour to the 45th meridian time. The ship was rolling heavily again. Weather was cloudy with strong southwest winds, force 7, and rough seas that broke over our deck. Dishes clattered all over the galley, the noise, a concern to the captain and mates.

Yesterday, I worked with the captain using a sextant to determine our position. He complimented me, again, and said I was doing well at navigation.

The gale force winds and heavy seas were causing the clinometer to register a roll of more than 25 deg. For a moment, I thought we were going over. Our position was latitude 47 deg. 12 min., longitude 47 deg., 21 min. AB Kardos reported sick with fever and was told to remain in bed. Deitz and I were assigned his watch.

At 3:45 p.m. the captain sighted a vessel abaft our port beam, about 7 miles off, steering a course parallel to our own. It looked like a Liberty ship heading for the same destination as ours. A battle drill was ordered. Battle stations were manned.

At 5:30 p.m. the bearing of the other vessel changed and she proceeded to head toward us. No signals were observed, but the vessel seemed to be going at a rate of about a half knot slower than us. We were making close to 11 knots. Our crew held their battle stations for more than an hour.

The next day, the same vessel was following dead astern, about six miles. The skipper thought her instruments were out of order, or she was unable to obtain a time check. He said, he was glad to be of help, but preferred to be alone. He regarded company, any company, with suspicion.

Saturday, December 19, clocks were advanced one hour to 15th meridian time. During the night we ran into dense fog, but continued on the same course. A fresh, but strong southwesterly breeze came up later and the vessel took breaking seas on deck.

Lt. Colwin and the captain called the armed guard on deck and gave them a serious talk saying, they observed some of the men were growing slack and indifferent. They emphasized the guard must keep a sharp lookout for the safety of the ship and all aboard. They were told to change their ways, or the captain and lieutenant would have to take more severe action. In the afternoon, the following Liberty ship was no longer observed.

Monday, December 21, clocks were advanced one hour to Greenwich time. Occasional snow flurries during the day, but the wind moderated with heavy seas and swells. The ship rolled easily, the sky was overcast, and the day passed uneventfully.

Deitz and I noted the courage of the ship's engineers, including the engine cadets, the oilers and wipers, in fact, all those known as the "Black Gang," who worked below. We were in dangerous waters. Lookouts were posted on deck. Submarines were certainly in the area. A torpedo hit would likely kill everyone on duty in the engine room. Yet those men, uncomplaining and unhesitating, day after day, night after night, went below to tend the engines.

In an emergency, we, deck cadets, could scramble to a lifeboat or a raft. No such opportunity existed for the engineers. We never discussed this with Tom or Jack, but we admired their courage.

Working with the bo'sun today, I saw him do a strange thing. I was tidying up the paint locker, when he came in with a white bread he had gotten somehow from the galley. Seated on a stool, the bo'sun cut off the ends of the bread and slowly poured the grey ship's paint through the bread, straining the paint. He then drank the residue from the pan and a few moments later, got up and calmly went about his business.

Wednesday, December 23, thirty-two days at sea since leaving

Balboa, Canal Zone. Dense fog today with medium to fresh northwesterly breeze.

An azimuth, later, found another sudden increase of error and deviation of our ship's compasses, causing real concern regarding our true course. The captain hoped for fair weather to get a sight and check our position. The compasses were not dependable now and the weather was miserable with rain, hail, cold, and wind squalls.

I dressed for my watch, 12 midnight to 4:00 a.m.with a sweatshirt, heavy woolen shirt, reversable jacket with a hood, raincoat, woolen stockings, boots, khaki pants, and two pairs of gloves.

The following day, I continued to stand the 12 to 4 watch with Mr. Kemp, the 2nd mate. The weather continued miserable, more cold, fog and rain. The mate told me there was no change of plans. We should be in Capetown, South Africa, in about a week. We moved the clocks ahead one hour.

Tonight was Christmas Eve. I spent part of the day painting Christmas cards, for the captain, and one for each table in the officers and crew's mess and received plaudits from the officers and crew. The cards looked professional.

Mr. Pruitt gave the cadets, each, a carton of cigarettes and gifts to the mates and Sparks. Everyone on board talked about home tonight, musing over Christmas dinners, trees and family get togethers. We were expecting a big spread tomorrow, and everyone will be dressing for dinner.

Friday, Christmas Day. The day began overcast, as usual, but the sea moderated somewhat. Slight swells and the vessel rolled gently. Fine weather at last! We were able to get a sight and found our position, latitude 44 deg. 8 min. south, longitude 20 deg. 38 min. east, pretty much on course.

At dinner, the captain and the mates appeared in dress blues and the cadets, in fresh khakis. Even the engineers looked tidy in clean dungarees and white shirts.

The steward's department had prepared an outstanding

Christmas dinner. A friendly spirit prevailed on board. Everyone seemed happy and contented.

The captain read a message to the crew from the Minister of War Transport of the British Admiralty, congratulating all seamen of the allied nations for doing an outstanding job in bringing supplies to Great Britain and helping to win the war against Nazism.

The skipper also expressed his thanks to all the crew for their help and cooperation during the trip. He wished each and every one a merry Christmas. We cadets, gave Hutchinson, our messman, two cartons of cigarettes.

The albatrosses that followed us for so many days are now gone. I wondered if that augured well, or not. I had fed them every day and somehow their presence was comforting.

Sunday, December 27, a fine, clear day with gentle southeasterly winds. The captain and mates tried to check deviation and error in our compasses. We were traveling a northerly route and they swung the ship several times from west to east, estimating the error and deviation. Finally, the captain set the course at north 20 deg. east and we zigzagged 30 deg. to each side.

Sparks received a message today that these are particularly dangerous waters as we approach Capetown. We have been zigzagging all night now changing course every six minutes. There was rising tension aboard ship, because of increased danger of submarines, and anticipation of being in Capetown on Tuesday.

CHAPTER V

South Africa

Monday, December 28, 1:15 p.m. we sighted aircraft, distinctly marked RSAAF, Royal South African Air Force. It was a welcome sight. They flew over us time and time again. The captain told me to hoist the American flag, while Simmons, the navy signalman, hoisted our call letters. The aircraft flew so low, we could see their crews waving greetings to us.

At about 4:00 p.m. we sighted another vessel inshore, bound eastward. Captain Norman could make out her call letters. She was the SS Mohegan with his friend Captain Homer Callas on the bridge.

We took soundings and Mr. Kemp told me to act as officer in charge. I made a perfect cast of the lead and we registered 68 fathoms with a sandy bottom. Mr. Kemp acted as a sailor. He heaved up the lead and said, "Yes, sir, good cast."

At 5:15 p.m. the bow lookout sighted land. It was the mountain eastward of Cape Agulhas. At 10:00 p.m Cape Agulhas, the southernmost part of Africa, was abeam.

Ever since leaving the Canal Zone, Mr. Pruitt had been fishing.

He succeeded in getting a meat hook from the galley. He tied a white rag around it, rove a line through the eye and then threw the hook over the side. It made a good lure. But day after day, as he pulled the hook up, it was empty, and he got a good deal of ribbing from the crew. They called it Pruitt's porpoise.

Today, Mr. Pruitt had a strike. An AB helped him haul in the line. He had caught a 20 pound barracuda. The fish had teeth like a dog. It was firm fleshed and tasty. We had a wonderful dinner of fresh barracuda. Mr. Pruitt was the ship's hero tonight.

We proceeded during the night steering by the stars. The compass was absolutely unreliable again.

The John Drayton arrived Capetown, South Africa, Tuesday, December 29, 1942 at 9:55 a.m. Total sailing time since leaving Balboa was 37 days, 3 hours, and 8 minutes. We had traveled 9,106 miles at an average speed of 10.2 knots.

We had crossed the equator, north to south; traversed the entire west coast of South America; sailed around Cape Horn, almost to the Antartic; crossed the South Atlantic; experienced extreme temperatures, very hot to very cold, rough to monstrous seas and arrived Capetown, with ship, cargo and crew intact. No small accomplishment.

I was looking forward to a good night's sleep, secure in the harbor. For the first time since leaving Panama, I was able to get completely undressed and slip between the sheets. There were no sleep interruptions, no seamen pounding at my door to call the watch, no restless scanning the sea seeking submarines, and no tension regarding a glimmer of light that might be showing from the blackout curtains.

Early the next morning we witnessed the fabled Capetown Table Mountain, a 4,000 foot plateau towering over the city, covered by wispy clouds, looking like a table set with crisp, white linen, and the napkins in disarray. A gentle breeze blew the clouds across the tabletop until they became a cascade down the side of the mountain. It was a majestic scene; the sun dazzling on the blue water, the golden city, bright in its welcome, and the bold mountain.

I went ashore with Kellegrew, Sparks, Deitz, the navy lieutenant and several gunners. Tom and I walked uptown and met the captain and the purser at the agent's office. They gave us each a draw of $50.00, roughly 13 South African pounds.

First, we got haircuts, and then went sightseeing in town. I was eager to get news of the war and found some back issues of Capetown newspapers and the Natal Daily News.

I learned, sadly, that "the Nazis persisted in their war against the Jews. Apparently, two million Jews had been exterminated in Poland. Allied governments condemned the Nazi systematic extermination of Europe's Jews and warned that those responsible would face retribution after the war."

News of Stalingrad indicated that "the battle was still raging as the Germans struggled to free their Sixth Army, trapped in the city. Winter had set in and the Russians launched an offensive which crumbled the Italian line and opened a gap in the German defenses."

Reports from North Africa were encouraging. "Rommel was in retreat and Britain's General Montgomery was being hailed as a hero."

Capetown was a beautiful city with parks, department stores, several movie houses, dance halls, plenty of shops, large and small, some run by Indians. There were hundreds of uniforms on the streets. We did a little shopping, but had to get back to the ship by 5:00 p.m. to move to the east pier for fuel and water.

The mate decided that a gangway watch was necessary and I volunteered so that an AB could go ashore. At 7:00 p.m. the 2nd mate, Mr. Kemp, went ashore. The skipper returned about 10:00 p.m. and relieved me of the watch. I got dressed again and went back ashore, but the town was blacked out and closed down. I went back to the ship at about 2:00 a.m. and had spent only about $30.00 in Capetown.

Two members of the steward department Chandler and Turner, returned to the ship, drunk. They were arguing in front of Captain Norman's door. Then Chandler pounded on the door and shouted, "Come on out Captain!"

There was no response. He pounded on the door again. "Come on out Captain!" The captain came out with a .38 caliber revolver strapped to his waist and asked, "What seems to be the trouble?" Chandler and Turner disappeared in the darkness.

Thursday, December 31, New Year's Eve. We moved the ship to the Degaussing range and adjusted the compasses. The skipper, lieutenant, and Sparks were busy all day attending naval conferences. By 12:00 midnight, the 2nd mate had not yet returned.

The following morning, by 7:00 a.m. the last member of the crew returned to the ship, with the exception of Mr. Kemp. Our vessel was ready to sail with a convoy at 10:00 a.m., but we were forced to drop out because the 2nd mate had failed to return. The captain signaled ashore to that effect and was told to stand by. The convoy would sail without us.

At 4:55 p.m. Mr. Kemp returned to the ship. He was brought aboard by a naval patrol launch, but the captain was told that we were too late to join the convoy. We would be routed, independently, to Durban, South Africa, to meet up with the convoy there.

Saturday, January 2, 6:06 a.m. we departed Capetown for Durban. Our noon position was latitude 34 deg., 30 min. south; longitude 18 deg., 45 minutes east, speed 10.2 knots.

The vessel sailed coastwise, only 16 miles offshore, with strong northwesterly winds and rough, heavy, following seas. The doors were dogged down and we took heavy seas on deck. The captain attempted to zigzag at times, but found it unsafe as dangerous seas broke over the deck when changing course. Planes were overhead constantly, and our guns were manned.

Morale and spirits aboard were at a low ebb. We had missed the convoy and were forced to run alone. Even loud mouth Chandler, the cook, was subdued. The 2nd mate picked at his food at breakfast. No one had spoken to him since he sobered up.

Tuesday, January 5, we were now about 10 miles offshore, zigzagging constantly against a strong three knot current. The wind and sea were moderating.

Wednesday, January 6, arrived Durban early this morning. I

stood by the engine telegraph and bell book and rang off the engines just in time to catch breakfast at 8:10 a.m.

Captain Norman met privately in his quarters with Mr. Kemp. We could imagine what transpired. The 2nd mate had been drinking ashore, and his lateness endangered the ship and crew. We were sure the captain laid him out.

The skipper went ashore soon after meeting with Mr. Kemp and returned almost immediately with the news we were pulling out in convoy at 3:00 p.m. The convoy had been waiting for us to arrive.

From the bridge, Durban looked like a handsome city. Houses, right down to the strand of beach, glistened white in the sunshine. There was no liberty, of course, but we were not sorry we could not get ashore. The end of the trip was in sight and we looked forward to getting to the Persian Gulf, unloading and returning home.

At 2:56 p.m., Departure. We are in a 12 vessel convoy. Five ships across, two deep, we were #43, two ships behind the commodore. We proceeded on a course of 80 deg., speed 8.9 knots, with moderate southwesterly breeze, moderate southwesterly sea, and passing clouds overhead. The vessel rolled gently.

Friday, January 8, 5:00 p.m. Our three British destroyer escort vessels left and returned to Durban. 6:00 p.m. a message from the commodore, signal flags flying, and the first vessels dispersed from the convoy. 7:30 p.m., final dispersal, and the ships scatter like a covey of quail. We were now running alone on a course of 75 deg. true. The William Patterson and Caesar Rodney were far off our port beam.

We continued to zigzag. Sparks brought a message to the captain indicating, unsettled weather ahead, a cyclone north of the Mozambique channel, heading southeast toward Madagascar.

The barometer was falling, 29.76. There was brilliant lightning ahead. The wind shifted to the southeast, but we soon saw fair weather clouds. Apparently, the disturbance passed to the southeast and the John Drayton is a fair weather ship again.

At 1:00 p.m. the engines were stopped for minor adjustments

for about 15 minutes. It seemed like an interminable length of time. The armed guard and cadets stood by their gun stations.

The weather was hot now and we took to sleeping on deck. The #3 hatch cover looked like a barracks, with cots lined up. During dark nights, sailors crept around, peering into sleeping faces, to be sure to wake the proper watch.

Temperature in the engine room registered 125 degrees, and over 90 degrees on deck. I remembered, seasons in the southern hemisphere are opposite from those in the northern hemisphere. January is mid-summer here, and as we approached the equator, the heat became even more oppressive.

Some crew members who were ashore in Capetown, reported they were told it would be long weeks and hot weather, while unloading our cargo in the Persian Gulf. The news was interesting, but I was surprised at the crew. Disclosing the name of the ship, cargo, and destination, was in violation of everything we had been told. "Loose lips, sink ships!"

We saw a rainbow tonight, about 11:00 p.m., the first I've ever seen at night. The moon was half full and very bright. The ship continued on an easterly course, zigzagging day and night.

We cadets have been busy with our studies and duties. Captain Norman allows me to use his sextant regularly and today I took a sight and a bearing with the azimuth mirror. I worked out the problem and brought the results to him on the bridge. He looked at it, smiled and said, "Captain Rosen, you can enter those figures in the log book and sign my name." It made my day. Sparks called me the ship's "aggravator."

I had been working with ABs, Ed Soderberg and Nick Tobiassen who patiently were teaching me knots and splices. I reciprocated by trying to explain navigation. Tom and Jack say they are becoming proficient in the engine room, and feel they could handle the duties of a third assistant engineer.

We have been in the Indian Ocean since leaving Capetown and the Cape of Good Hope. Today, January 14 the sea is like glass. Thousands of flying fish are around us and the sky is as clear as an agate.

At 11:15 p.m. an oil fuel line was carried away and the engines stopped. Repairs were started immediately, and completed in 31 minutes. According to the chief engineer, it was a defective installation of an oil line in the shipyard. Armed guard and cadets stood by gun stations feeling vulnerable, like sitting ducks on a pond of circling sharks.

Saturday, January 16, our noon position 5 deg., 20 min. south, 58 deg., 12 min. east, light westerly breezes with smooth seas and passing cumulus clouds, fine weather during the entire day. The captain called a fire and boat drill and the crew was mustered at their stations. Battle station drills were held, all guns were manned, ready for action.

Later that day, the chief mate assigned me to work with Mr. Pruitt, the 3rd mate, to check contents of the lifeboats and rafts again to be certain each boat was equipped with a set of sails and oars, pemmican, a flare gun and flares, a water cask with fresh water, a bucket, hatchet, and watertight container with matches. (Pemmican, in small floatation cans is a rich, highly nutritious food, made of ground coconut, ground nuts, raisins, fat and sugar.)

Sunday, January 17, 1943. Today, four months since I signed on the John Drayton, is a troublesome day for all of us. We are running at reduced speed because of serious defects in the engine room and according to the chief engineer, there is a question of whether we can make it to Abadan in the Persian Gulf. The captain and chief discussed how to conserve the engines and decided to run at reduced speed and stop the zigzag. There is more tension now aboard ship. Slowing down and stopping the zigzag, makes us an easier target.

At 7:00 p.m. we cross the equator from south to north. The weather is hot and oppressive. There is constant work below on the engines.

Captain Norman was spending more time on the bridge now. It seems to me he is always there, scanning the horizon with his glasses, or checking the compass. On those rare times he was not on the bridge, if we needed him in a hurry, we had a primitive, but effective, way of calling him. We jumped three times on the deck over his head. He'd be up on the bridge in 10 seconds. Mr. Pruitt timed him.

Friday, January 22, gentle easterly winds and a slight sea, passing clouds, made for fine weather. We picked up speed, the vessel was zigzagging again. We are bucking a current, setting north northwest, a half mile per hour, coming out of the Red Sea and Gulf of Aden. Approaching the Arabian coast, the ship continues to zigzag.

The following day, during my relief at the wheel, the lookout shouted, "Spout, two points off the starboard beam!"

The captain immediately ordered "Hard right." The ship swung slowly while the skipper and the mate scanned the surface again and again.

The spout worried the captain. When I came up on the bridge at 8:00 p.m. to stand lookout watch, he was still there, carefully watching the sea. The spout could have been a porpoise, flying fish, or the plume of a periscope, and he was taking no chances. He gave me a pair of binoculars and warned me to keep a sharp lookout.

Saturday, January 23, 4:00 a.m. We pass around Ras Al Hadd Point, about 40 miles off. At daylight, high mountains of Oman were seen at a distance and the vessel now is in the Gulf of Oman.

About 6:00 a.m. we sight two felucca fishing vessels and regard them with suspicion. Sparks pointed out that although they are ancient type sailboats, they can carry modern radios. He said, they could easily be in touch with enemy submarines.

I have not been feeling too well the past few days. Sparks and the lieutenant were also complaining. The mate believes we have a touch of tropical fever.

Today, it looks as though two of my three bets will pay off. On entering Guantanamo Bay, I bet the 1st assistant engineer, 8 to 5, that we were headed for the Persian Gulf. He was very sure that since it was so obvious we were heading to the Persian Gulf, we would certainly go elsewhere. I was willing to give him odds, so sure that the navy wasn't that slick. This morning at breakfast, he asked me whether I wanted my money in American dollars or British pounds.

Last week, Sparks, Tommy, and I bet a drink on estimating the day of arrival. I called it January 27, Sparks, 28, and Tommy, 29. So far, it looks like 27. My third bet is a crew pool. Every man chipped in fifty cents and picked one number out of 60 out of a hat. Each number is the minute of the hour that we arrive and the engines are rung off. The man who picked that minute, wins thirty dollars. My number is 30.

We had a short, but heavy rain storm last night during my turn at the wheel. The captain relieved me long enough so I could get a raincoat. It was another indication of his kindness and consideration.

CHAPTER VI

Persian Gulf

The following morning a vessel was sighted on a bearing approaching us. All guns were manned. At 9:00 a.m. signals were exchanged and it was determined to be British gun boat #J179. At 11:36 a.m. a shore light was observed bearing north, indicating we are entering the Persian Gulf, leaving the Gulf of Oman.

I am feeling better now, but the 2nd assistant engineer has come down with a chill. The lieutenant mentioned this morning, that navy gunner Spellings was left in a Capetown hospital. I was not aware and had not missed him.

Working today with Flowers, the ship's carpenter, and the bo'sun, Deitz and I overhauled cargo blocks, getting the gear ready for unloading. The ship is proceeding up the Persian Gulf towards Abadan, Persia. We are no longer zigzagging.

Tuesday, January 26. Using the sextant and working with the chief mate, at 6:12 a.m. we get an excellent star fix and deviation of the compass observed by Polaris, Altair, and Deneb, Vega and Spica. Position is latitude 29 deg., 2 min., longitude 49 deg., 28 min. east. We are 22 miles from the light vessel. The error of the compass is 8 deg. and 30 min. east, the deviation is 6 min. east. We are steering 290 degrees, due to an allowance made for leeway and current.

At 8:15 a.m. the Shatt Al Arab light vessel is abeam, close on the portside and we proceed, as instructed by naval control in Durban, picking up the marked red and white buoys. At 12:16 the ship anchors in the examination anchorage in the Shatt Al Arab river. Sixty fathoms of chain go out. At 12:17, we are finished with engines, and AB Hudgins wins the ship's pool, collecting thirty dollars.

Soon, Royal Navy Lt. Harris came aboard for routine check of cargo, but was unable to offer any definite information regarding how long we will remain at anchor. There are about 15 vessels here, some having been here as long as one month. Lt. Harris explained why there are so many ships anchored here at this time. He said, more vessels are now arriving safely in the Persian Gulf. Previously, a large percentage of the ships were sunk, en route, and never reached here.

He said, it is expected the Allies will win control of North Africa soon, and, ships will be routed from the East coast of the U.S. through the Mediterranean, into the Aegean, through the Dardenelles, to the Black Sea and probably to the Russian port, Sevastopol. He thought the Persian Gulf would not be used much longer as an unloading area.

There will be no shore leave, as we are anchored some twenty miles from shore. Total distance, we travelled New York to Abadan, 17,260 miles, average speed 10.1 knots, hours steaming 71 days, 4 hours and 54 minutes. All aboard agree the John Drayton is a "worthy ship".

The chief mate has broken sea watches. The mates now stand 8 hours on and 16 off. Ordinary seamen stand regular watches and the armed guard remains on duty at all times.

Close watch is kept on the signal station for a signal indicating an air raid. By day, the signal is a black flag and by night, it's dot, dash, dot, by horn.

It's a little community of ships we joined here. Crews visit each other, to swap news, stories, libraries, etc. A few cadets have come aboard already, and I met one I knew from the Academy.

We expect our sojourn in the Persian Gulf will be a long one. The mate is going to have us painting, chipping, and scraping tomorrow.

I went aloft today in the bo'sun's chair, while working with Eddie Soderberg and Flowers, the ship's carpenter, greasing blocks. It was quite a feeling, hanging by a piece of rope 60 feet above the deck, but I'm getting to be an old hand at it.

The weather here is good. Winter in the Persian Gulf has the snap and sparkle of an autumn day at home. By mid day, the sun warms up and sweaters can be discarded. Nights are like the famed Arabian Nights, when the sky is colored from pink to deep purple. Sleeping at night is wonderful. It's great climbing between clean sheets and sleeping steadily for eight hours without having someone shaking you to go out on watch.

British planes appeared today, flying low, checking on our deck cargo.

Mort Deitz and I have been scraping the top sides and decks. We scrape off the rust, then put a thin coat of foul smelling fish oil over the surface. By the end of the day, I am certain that both of us would get seats on the subway. The mate explained the battle against rust at sea is constant. If unchecked, salt water eats through the ship's plates in a matter of months.

After fish oiling, Deitz and I applied a coat of red lead. When it dried, we painted the area battleship gray, which matched the color of the ship.

A Russian plane, plainly marked with the red star, came over to entertain us. It started looping and roaring over the mast, so low, we could see the cracks in his paint-work. We had our guns trained on him, taking no chances, until he disappeared into the clouds. The Russian was flying the same type plane, as we carry on our deck, the Douglas A20 bomber, a beautiful, speedy, and maneuverable job.

Saturday, January 30, 4:00 p.m. Lt. Harris came on board with orders, "The vessel is to proceed to Abadan, on high water, tomorrow morning, to begin unloading". He also brought us the latest news bulletins of the war. "Some Germans are beginning to surrender at Stalingrad and colossal losses have been inflicted on the German army."

"In Poland the Germans were surprised by the resistance of Jews in the Warsaw ghetto."

"Churchill and Roosevelt met in Casablanca to plan the next moves in the war."

"On the whole," Lt. Harris said "the news was good."

At 6:00 p.m. Persian Gulf pilot, H. Sheref and his pilot apprentice, came on board. They are to sleep aboard the John Drayton so that we may get an early start in the morning.

I was assigned to find sleeping quarters for Josif, the pilot apprentice. He speaks English quite well and tells me he has to study, and act as an apprentice, for two and a half years before getting his pilot license.

Josif had some strange misinformation. He said, there are many American soldiers in Iraq and they are also fighting alongside British and Indian troops in Russia. American wounded are being sent to Bombay and Basra. The Allied troops, not the Russians, he said, are responsible for stopping Hitler's offensive in the Caucasus.

Getting back to pilotage, Josif pointed out that Turkish ships, according to International Rules of the Road do not blow whistles, because a whistle means fire in Turkey, so to avoid confusion, they use gongs. Josif gave me a pilotage certificate in Arabic, and said if he could find time, he would go ashore with us in Abadan.

Like all the others we've met, Josif's ambition is to visit the United States. He has no use at all for the British, and can't understand why the Americans are "fighting to save the British." Americans are extremely popular, he said, and get along with the native population, contrary to the "bloody Limeys". He was interested in our cadet training and wanted to know what subjects we study and how long it takes before we become licensed officers in the merchant marine, or officers in the navy.

Sunday, January 31, 1943. 4:30 a.m. all in readiness for leaving. 5:40 a.m. receive signal to proceed. 6:37 a.m. cross the bar and proceed up the river. 7:40 a.m. pass the control vessel. 12:30 p.m. stop off Abadan, 12:31, anchor 45 fathoms of water. 12:39 p.m. finished with engines, await the quarantine doctor.

Josif and the pilot are taken ashore in a small launch. We are not permitted ashore. The doctor from the Anglo-Iranian oil company hospital is expected to vaccinate the crew for smallpox.

The following day, we docked at about 4:30 p.m. and before all lines were made fast, the first plane was already ashore, by means of a 200 ton floating crane. The Sherman tanks soon followed. There is, obviously, great anxiety for our cargo. As for us, we are very pleased. Finally, after more than four months and over 17,000 miles we are, at last, unloading in Abadan, Persia.

Thursday, February 4. We left Abadan this morning, and proceeded about 10 miles upstream to Harta Point, the explosive anchorage. There, crews unloaded #1, #3 and #4 holds which carried explosives and ammunition. Harta was a safe point, far enough from the city of Abadan, in case of an explosion.

Tommy and I had gone ashore in Abadan. We visited the Douglas airfield where our planes were being assembled. We talked with U.S. army pilots and aircraft workers and met two Russian pilots with whom we communicated by hand gestures.

They were both lieutenants who had seen action over Moscow. The younger one, 21, had been shot down and wounded twice. They were disciplined and the picture of good health.

We asked the Russians to go to Abadan with us, but by tugging and yanking on his ear, one indicated, Abadan was out of bounds. The Russians had great respect for American pilots and they showed us by gestures that our planes were the best.

On return to the ship we were informed two of our messmen, Chandler and Prior are in prison in an army stockade for unruliness and drunkenness. The captain tried several times to get them released, but was told of an army order, "any merchant seaman in prison, must remain there until his ship is ready to sail."

Everyone on board is disappointed in the mail service. It's been over four months since we left the States, and no one has received any mail. We turned letters over to the navy at Guantanamo and Capetown for mailing. I hope the letters got through, but, to date, I've heard nothing from home. All of us expect mail will catch up with us while we're here in the Persian Gulf.

Today, Lincoln's birthday, we are still anchored at Harta Point. There is no news of when we'll move or where. I was ashore several times, but there isn't very much to see or do. The country is flat, barren, sandy, and extremely poor. The people seem to know only one word, "bakshish", meaning, alms.

CHAPTER VII

Iran-Iraq

The town of Khorramshahr is only a short distance up the river and I walked there with Tommy, Ed Soderberg, Flowers, and George Bowman, another AB. We found many American soldiers there anxious to go home. The town is much the same as Abadan, dirty, run-down, with nothing much to do for amusement.

On board ship, we've been chipping, scraping, and painting. Except for the wait, it's not unpleasant here. The food is still good and the weather just right. There's much activity on the river. Ships moving in and out constantly. There are many liberty ships, the Rodney, Foster, Henry, Brown, Terry, Davis, Patterson, and others.

Today, Tuesday, February 16 marks five months since we signed on the John Drayton in Wilmington, North Carolina. We cadets, when not on duty, gather in Sparks' room near the radio shack to shoot the breeze and bemoan that we are still here anchored at Harta Point, with no idea of when we shall be leaving.

Sparks, handicapped with his heavy metal brace, has been forced to remain on board, since he would navigate only with difficulty if ashore. We reassure him, going ashore is not much fun anyway. Aside from the lack of entertainment, and no possible places to eat, one is constantly confronted by a horde of pitiful beggars crying, "bakshish, no mama, no papa, bakshish."

The following day we are surprised to see Chandler and Prior come aboard. They were released to Captain Norman's custody by the commanding officer of the U.S. staging area. Prior is subdued. Chandler is loudly demanding money, and stating the captain was responsible for his being in prison. Captain Norman said he would not log in charges, providing Chandler and Prior went to work, kept sober, and caused no further trouble, and also, that they did not go ashore again, at any time, during the vessel's stay in the Persian Gulf.

Washington's birthday, Monday, February 22. Still anchored at Harta Point. Mort Deitz and I are using our free time to work on our sea projects, and the mate has been keeping us busy wire brushing, red leading and gray painting the blackout ports. I've also been working on a stage over the side, red leading the bow.

The weather is usually fair, except for an occasional heavy dust storm, which covers the deck with a thick layer of desert dust. Frequent thunderstorms soon wash it clean.

The crew seems to suffer minor illnesses and our motor lifeboat is busy with trips to army doctors and dentists in Khorramshahr. Throughout the time we have been anchored in Harta Point, we, and the armed guard have been standing watches, and armed guard are posted on the ship to be certain no unauthorized persons gain entry.

At last, Thursday, February 25, 10:45 a.m. a barge is along side and two Arab gangs start slowly, discharging additional ammunition on to the barge from #1 #5 holds. Our ABs are at the winches. Slings are dropped into the holds, where they are loaded, and the ammunition is carefully discharged and stacked on the barge. The process is slow and repeated, again and again. Dietz and I have been standing by the chief mate, who is carefully overseeing the work.

The William Patterson, a Liberty ship, anchored astern of us during the night, and cadets were over to visit.

Ed Soderberg and Nick Tobiassen, ABs, always find time to teach me knots, splices, and seamanship. Ed is about 27 years old and has knocked around the world on all sorts of freighters. He knows sailing and is ready always to lend a hand.

Nick is somewhat older, a Dane, who had gone to sea, almost as soon as he could walk. He sailed on everything, including wind jammers and knows all there is to know about the duties of a seaman. Even the bo'sun turns to Nick for a hand with a wire splice or reaving a block. Nick typifies the legendary seaman, who busies himself off watch, mounting a board with sample knots, or whittling wooden whistles.

Between Ed and Nick, I learned seamen's lore, which is never fully explained in textbooks. One day, they spent hours teaching me how to make a monkey's fist, the weighted ball at the end of a heaving line.

Monday, March 1. Two barges, loaded with ammunition discharged from our ship, are towed away. Later that morning, messman Prior cut his finger severely. He is taken to the doctor for treatment, along with Hudgins and Bowman, ABs, who have been complaining of feeling ill.

Another barge comes alongside later in the afternoon and ammunition continues to be unloaded from #1 and #5 holds.

Saturday, March 6, the loaded ammunition barge is towed away and we are advised to move to Abadan, where we take on fuel and 120 tons of fresh water. We remained at the dock until the following day. The crew was permitted ashore to the seaman's club.

The following day we are back at anchor at Harta Point. Suddenly, on board, there is a loud explosion in the fire chamber of the boiler room. Fortunately, no one is injured. Orders are, however, the vessel is to remain at anchor until investigation of the damage is done. After assessment, it was established there is only minor damage and repairs are completed quickly. Some of the crew, however, expressed concern to the chief engineer regarding the safety of the ship, pointing out that several accidents and explosions have occurred in the engine room.

We have been in the Persian Gulf about seven weeks now, and

there is virtually no opportunity to allay the growing restiveness regarding our delayed return to the States. Liberty ashore is dull and some crew members return after only a short spell. They are concerned that most of our general cargo is still on board. The quality and quantity of our food is deteriorating and the weather is getting warmer, adding to anxiety and discomfort.

Wednesday, March 10. River pilot on board, and we have orders to proceed to the dock in Khorramshahr. At 1:00 a.m. the ordinary seaman woke me and I went forward with the 2nd mate to help haul in the anchors. In pitch darkness, we hauled in both chains, hosed them down, and we finally depart Harta Point. We got into Khorramshahr just about dawn, after anchoring outside for several hours.

Stevedores, waiting at the dock, are newly arrived, black American troops. They are fine, healthy looking men, who although green about handling cargo, are intelligent and willing to learn. The dour chief mate hopes they will do better than he expects.

There are frequent delays at all hatches because of the shortage of trucks on the dock to remove the cargo, and as a result, the mate says, "From 1:00 a.m. to 6:00 a.m. is breakfast, from 6:00 a.m. to 12:00 noon is lunch, and noon to 6:00 p.m. is dinner. The clock goes around again, 6:00 p.m. to 12:00 midnight starts with lunch."

It's a long, slow process, not because of the inefficiency of the stevedores, but simply because of the shortage of trucks.

However, with each sling of cargo that goes ashore from our ship, morale of the crew improves. There is talk now that we should be homeward bound inside of three weeks. It wouldn't surprise me though, if it is sooner. Just give these stevedores enough trucks and they will get the job done in a very short time.

The mate explained that our Douglas A20 bombers were assembled at the airfield near Abadan and flown to the Soviet Union. Our Sherman tanks, he said, were put on flat cars and taken across Iran by railroad to Russia, and our general cargo will be taken by truck over new roads, built by American and British engineers, to the Russian border.

He was glum, as usual, about getting the required number of

trucks to complete unloading the ship before the end of March or early April.

I spent afternoons studying cargo stowage and unloading, from textbooks and also by carefully observing the rigging, and the operation of the booms and the winches.

During the evenings, I transcribed my notes on Sparks' typewriter while he loafed around, occasionally imparting some bits of information he had picked up at sea. He explained, for example, why men's jackets, today, have three or four buttons sewn on the sleeve. He said the custom came from the old British navy.

Heavy brass buttons were sewn on the sleeves of midshipmen's jackets. Midshipmen, in those days, were about twelve years old, and the buttons prevented them from using their sleeves to wipe their noses.

On Saturday, March 13, as I was planning to go ashore with Tommy, the captain and the mate advised me to get back as soon as possible as I would have to stand the 2nd mate's watch. Mr. Kemp had not yet returned to the ship and was due to stand watch from 10:00 p.m. to 6:00 a.m. overseeing unloading cargo, tending to the ship's lines, and checking winches.

Tommy and I went ashore to the army PX where we bought some toothpaste and candy and came back to the ship soon afterward. Mr. Kemp got back to the ship at 9:00 p.m., somewhat unsteady, but able to stand his watch.

Days passed uneventfully and sporadic discharge of cargo continued. Barometer is registering 30 degrees, air temperature 72. The weather is fair.

I have been working on my sea project and the mate asked me to watch the hatches from 8:00 to 12:00 to see that the longshoremen don't abuse the gear, and that the unloading of cargo proceeds in good order.

The chief steward has reported that messman Chandler has not appeared for the past several days, apparently, he's back in prison. On Thursday, March 25 the captain was advised that Chandler is being held in prison and must remain there until the vessel is ready to sail.

Robert Browning, wiper, reported on board after being missing for three days. Ashore, he had been robbed and beaten and his clothing taken. He came aboard in only his undershorts.

The Anglo-Iranian oil company towered over the Abadan Khorramshahr area and the smell of oil was everywhere. The town "streets" were rutted clay and natives, dressed in burlap sacks, or tattered sheets, jostled and pushed to get close to us. It was particularly dangerous at night and it was not unusual for crew members to be robbed, beaten, and have items of clothing stolen. It was never advisable for anyone to go ashore at night, nor to go alone.

Tom Kellegrew and I stopped by the bazaar in Abadan, one day. It was a busy place, surrounded by small shops and stalls. Merchants displayed their wares of rugs, jewelry, shoes, and cloth. Most of the shoppers were natives, who it seemed, never purchased anything. Only when an American seaman, or GI, stopped by one of the stalls, was there any business activity.

We stopped at the butcher's to watch a man buy meat. What must have been a skinned sheep or goat, was hanging in the hot sun, covered with flies. The buyer pointed to part of the leg, and the butcher hacked it off. The flies were hardly disturbed. Then the man put the unwrapped meat, still swarming with flies, into his cloth bag, and went on his way. We had been told that comparatively few natives lived beyond the age of 30, and we could easily understand why.

Around the bazaar, native mud huts were crowded into narrow, winding alleys. Some families sat in the doorways, while children roamed the streets. On our way back to the ship, we were surrounded by the usual crowd of beggars. A GI in a jeep stopped for us, we jumped in, and he took us to the motor pool, then back to the ship.

At the Abadan bazaar, Tom and I had our pictures taken by a photographer who had a stall. Tom was seated in a chair in the middle of the street, and I stood next to him. We waited while the photographer developed the film, two copies cost ten rials, which was equivalent to about thirty cents, U.S.

While anchored at Harta Point, native bum boats were alongside daily from early morn to dusk, trying to sell us straw hats, carpets, hand-made shoes, blankets, and other items. Most of the vendors were children who had picked up some words of English and in the morning we would be awakened by young voices shouting, "Hey, Johnny, hey, Johnny, you buy shoes, you buy hats."

A general fracas ensued if a sailor indicated that he wanted to buy something. The vendors then shouted, "Mine, mine, buy mine, Johnny!" and they raced forward in their boats to be first. For 20 rials I bought a pair of Persian sandals, the kind that curl up at the toe.

Later, for one rial, a bum boat took me to Iraq, just on the other side of the river. It was a beautiful day and I walked along one of the irrigation canals for about a half mile, and suddenly, I was in the midst of a small village of the usual mud huts.

Several men were squatting on the ground talking and were surprised to see me. I held my hands up, palms out, and kept nodding and smiling as I walked toward them.

The men stood up in a half circle and one smiled at me and extended his hand. We shook hands solemnly. He was friendly and gestured to show me around the village. We were followed by kids, and dogs, and chickens and soon the village square was crowded. Several women, holding bundles of what appeared to be laundry, were peeking out from behind their huts.

My friend pointed to tall palms planted near the canal. "Dates," he said, proud of his English. I nodded and repeated "dates." He then pointed to the earth, the sky and a tree and said the Arabic word for each.

The Arab then spoke to someone in a hut, and in a moment, a woman came out carrying some greens in an earthen bowl and flat bread which she handed to him. He urged me to have some, but I pointed to my stomach and showed him that I was full. We had been warned by the army doctor not to eat any native food because of dysentery.

Soon, I felt it was time for me to leave, and I extended my

hand, which my friend grasped firmly. I wanted to give him something to show my appreciation for his hospitality, and I remembered that I had a small pocket knife. I handed it to him and he was very pleased. He examined the knife carefully, showed it to his friends, opening both blades, and turning it over. Then he shook my hand again. I waved when I got back to the canal and they were still standing, looking toward me.

These were simple farmers, who possessed the dignity of people who lived off the soil. They knew hard work and they shared generously. They, certainly, were different from the city beggars, who begged "bakshish, Johnny, bakshish."

The black soldiers worked on discharging our ship day and night. #2, #3 and #4 holds are cavernous on a Liberty ship and it was amazing to see what they contained. Jeeps, trucks, flour, bags of cement, canned goods, cases of beer, cartons of small arms, blankets, boots. The stevedores were efficient. There were no delays. Apparently, the needed trucks were obtained. The cargo moved on to the dock, and it was soon whisked away. Our steward department welcomed the black soldiers, like cousins, and the coffee maker in the crew's galley perked day and night.

Sunday, March 28, the vessel left the dock at Khorramshahr and anchored upstream. The vacant berth was used immediately by another vessel to begin unloading. Two gangs continued working on the John Drayton, slowly unloading holds #1 and #2 onto a barge. Finally, complete discharge on March 31.

Two members of the crew, Chandler and William Manley, oiler, who had been in the army prison, were discharged into the custody of Captain Norman. All members of the crew are refused liberty now. The doctor advised there is typhoid fever raging ashore, and it is taking many lives daily.

CHAPTER VIII

Homeward Bound

Thursday, April 1. Heave up anchor at 12:16 p.m. and turn the ship around in the river. At last, we are headed home, after more than two months in the Persian Gulf. The John Drayton and her crew, have safely delivered and discharged our cargo, planes, tanks, and supplies destined for the Russians, who are now defending Kharkov.

The planes will be flown to the Russian border by pilots, like those we met in Abadan. The tanks will be placed on railroad flat cars and carted across Iran to the Russian border, and the trucks laden down, will travel north on good, new roads built by British and American engineers. The crew now, is anxious to get home, but proud of having done the job.

The weather is fine and clear. We are making good time, 12.23 knots and we are heading for Bahrain, where we will get fuel for the homeward trip. Soon after we tie-up in Bahrain, we were joined by the Liberty ship, Cardinal Gibbons and there is talk of a convoy forming here.

The following day, we depart Bahrain at 6:56 a.m. and head

toward the assembly anchorage, where the convoy will be forming. The weather has turned bad. There are fresh, strong, northerly winds and rain squalls constantly during the day with heavy rain at about 9:00 p.m.

Captain Norman has received word of increased submarine warfare, particularly in the North Atlantic. In the last three weeks, at least 50 allied merchant ships have been sunk. Apparently, two convoys were attacked by a pack of U-boats, resulting in heavy losses. The captain has ordered increased lookout watch.

Sunday, April 4, dawns fine and clear. We are making good time toward the assembly anchorage. At about 11:00 a.m., we observe numerous vessels ahead of us, as the convoy is starting to get underway. We are late and the skipper increases speed while we exchange signals with the escort vessel, a British destroyer. We are granted permission to join the convoy as #34. The Liberty ship Caesar Rodney is #25, and at 1:30 p.m. the Cardinal Gibbons joins the convoy as #14.

Monday, April 5, the day is fine and clear. The sea is smooth. The temperature, however, is warming up. It is now 90 degrees. The convoy is made up of 18 vessels, but there is heavy smoke from a Polish transport. The captain and the chief mate are quite disturbed about it, and agree we would rather be by ourselves.

At 6:30 p.m. three blasts from tanker #24, meaning "man overboard." The tanker falls out of the column, and an escort proceeds to pick up the man.

Tuesday, April 6. In convoy, the Polish vessel is still making heavy smoke. 7:35 a.m., vessel Sudenholme, signals that she is unable to keep up with the convoy. The Commodore signals the John Drayton is to take her position, #33. Temperature is over 90 degrees, sea smooth, winds northerly, fine and clear.

4:15 p.m. signal from the commodore, "Convoy is to scatter". Each ship is to proceed to its destination independently. Our latitude is 23 deg. north, longitude 62 deg. east. We traveled in convoy from Bahrain to point of dispersal, 782 miles.

On board the John Drayton, we're back to routine. Mort Deitz and I are handling the blackouts, and I relieve the man at the wheel for dinner at 5:00 p.m. Tom and Jack are delighted to be back in the engine room, heading home at last.

Wednesday, April 7 the captain orders increased lookouts posted throughout the ship. I take the 8-12 watch with the 3rd mate and Deitz, the 12-4 watch with the 2nd mate. The day is fine and clear and the sea smooth.

At 8:44 a.m. the captain orders a battle drill. Firing practice follows with the 5" gun aft which does a good job, so do the 20 mm guns on the bridge. The 3 in. gun forward is only fair.

The barometer is steady at 29.90. The temperature, however, is warming up. It is now 92 degrees.

At 2:00 a.m. the following morning, the 2nd mate summoned the captain. He has seen a suspicious craft seeming to follow our ship. The captain, on the bridge, says it looks like a submarine and later, upon examination, he thinks it might be a raider. Lt. Colwin is called and at 4:51 all guns are manned and kept ready. The captain orders a course change from 190 degrees to 150 in order to observe any change of bearing of the following ship. The vessel finally disappears and we resume course at 190. At daylight, we observe the vessel to be the Cardinal Gibbons.

At noon, our position is latitude 15 deg., 6 min. north, longitude 61 deg., 16 min. east. Speed is 11.7 knots. The Cardinal Gibbons is off our port beam about 7 miles.

The John Drayton is empty, except for ballast, and riding high in the water. With rpm about 68, a slight vibration is felt on changing course, especially when the propeller is out of the water. Air temperature now is well over 90 and the captain has taken to sleeping on a cot on the bridge.

We are proceeding in the Arabian Sea approaching the equator. The wind is easterly, light, and variable. The Cardinal Gibbons is following on our port quarter making about the same speed, 11.58 knots.

Sunday, April 12, Bahrain Point to Capetown, South Africa. The weather is fair, with a light westerly wind and a slight swell, passing clouds. From 9:40 to 10:00 a.m. there is a sudden, heavy, westerly monsoon rain. Everyone on board is soaked. The weather is hot and the crew has now taken to sleeping on deck. At 4:00 p.m., we pass the equator, north to south.

Our food is now decidedly bad. The usual procedure after coming off watch is to go to the officers' mess and have a light snack before going to bed. Tonight, the snack was simply stale bread and coffee. The bread was covered with roaches. I swept the roaches aside, but because I was hungry, I ate the bread and had some coffee before hitting the sack. The crew is now looking forward, anxiously, to Capetown for fresh provisions and to mark another leg of the journey home. Complaints about the food are frequent, and there is more and more talk about the "belly robber," a new term for the chief steward.

Lookouts are on duty, constantly, throughout the ship, and strict blackout is observed. At this rate, the mate believes we should be in Capetown by April 23.

The next day at 8:00 p.m., we are abeam of the Seychelles Island group, which is about 200 miles to the west. The ship is turning 69 rpm and the vibration is strong at times.

About 7:00 p.m. we sight a vessel on the starboard beam. It appears to be hanging on and following us. The #5 gun is in readiness aft. At 8:00 p.m. the vessel slowly drops out of sight. It is very suspicious. The crew is alert and a sharp lookout is maintained.

Tom Kellegrew is now alternating watch with the third assistant engineer, and the chief is pleased with his performance. Mort Deitz and I are working navigation sights, routinely. I had a star fix which set our latitude at 11 deg., 30 min. south; longitude 57 deg., 20 min. east. A member of our armed guard Wolfe, ill, since we left Bahrain, is feeling better. He has not been able to say exactly what ails him. Apparently, it is nothing serious.

Friday, April 16 marks seven months since the John Drayton set out from Wilmington, North Carolina, and, today, puts us well on the way home.

The food situation is very bad. A satisfying meal is no more, and will be no more until Capetown. Stomach disorders are frequent on board. The whole crew is looking forward to Capetown, to a good meal, and possibly a good night's sleep in the harbor.

Mr. Pruitt, the 3rd mate, and the bo'sun have been fishing ever since we left Persia, but there is nary a bite.

We're averaging close to 12 knots. The weather is hot, approaching 100 degrees, but all hands are pleased. The end of June, if all goes well, should see us somewhere in the States.

According to our navigational fix, we are now passing about midway between Reunion Island and Madagascar. We are in the Indian Ocean. The barometer is holding steady at 30. The suspicious vessel, previously seen, is not seen again.

Saturday, April 17, we are off the southeast point of Madagascar. The wind is fresh northeasterly, rough following sea, barometer 29.95. At daybreak, we sight the Cardinal Gibbons ahead about 4 miles and holding her position. At about sunset, we run into a powerful lightning and thunderstorm. All hands are told to sleep inside in regular quarters. 9:00 p.m. teriffic electrical storm overhead, heavy southwest wind and rain. The weather clears about midnight.

Sunday, April 18, the day is cloudy and cold. Poor observation is obtained and we estimate our latitude at 27 deg., 30 min. south and longitude 68 deg., 20 min. east. Our speed has been cut down considerably. The engines have been slowed and we are down to 60 rpm due to the engine racing. The rpm were cut down to avoid possible damage. Jack Stadstad, standing watch with the 2nd assistant engineer, reports there is extreme vibration in the engine room as a result of the propeller coming out of the water and the racing engine.

Monday, April 19, overcast sky, strong easterly winds, and rough to heavy easterly and confused seas. The vessel is at reduced speed and racing madly. We are not able to obtain an observation because of cloud cover. The barometer is dropping steadily and it is anticipated that there is bad weather ahead. We hit heavy rain squalls from the east and strong winds from the southeast.

At 4:00 p.m. the barometer stops falling and the air is clearing in the west. Sparks notifies the captain a severe cyclone has passed astern of us. We had been anticipating a long and dreary night, but luckily the weather seems to be clearing. It begins to blow again before midnight, building to a southeasterly gale, but the ship behaves well.

Walking on deck is treacherous. The decks are slick. The waves wash over them and the high wind makes it difficult to maneuver to get to one's post. Lookouts are posted throughout the ship, and we are still zigzagging. The strong winds cause the captain to believe that we've been blown off course. We have not been able to get a sight for the last 36 hours and we are using dead reckoning to establish our position.

There is little food aboard, and tempers are short. This run, Bahrain to Capetown, day after day, seems the longest and the most dismal. It is still about 8 days until Capetown. The weather has changed and it is now chilly. All hands have moved indoors.

The following day, the weather moderated somewhat and we were able to get a star sight. Our position is 31 deg., 20 min. south, 40 deg., 20 min. east. We are on a course of 250 degrees and our speed is 9.5 knots. The weather has turned cold. It is now 74 degrees, the sea temperature is 76 degrees. The barometer is 29.90.

CHAPTER IX

Torpedoed!

The following day, April 21, our noon position leaves us still about 1,000 miles to go to Capetown. Our speed has increased to about 11 knots. The wind is fresh from southeast, with a rough sea. We are making fair time.

It is a clear, fine night with a full moon and we have retarded the clocks 1-1/2 hours to Capetown time, the 30th meridian. We are experiencing a strong, southeasterly current from the Mozambique Channel and the wind is increasing from the southeast with the apparent approach of an East Indian gale. We are steering 235, slightly to the right of the course, to compensate for the heavy wind and sea, abeam. Every half hour we steer 20 degrees to the right for 10 minutes, then 20 degrees to the left, in a zigzag pattern in the event anything is ahead.

At 6:20 p.m. bow lookouts Morris and an armed guard, report seeing a wake in the water passing from port to starboard, as if a fish or some object passed by. The captain calls Morris to the bridge and asks for details. The skipper thinks it may have been a torpedo. He instructs the crew to keep a very sharp lookout.

At this time, the mate is on the bridge standing his regular 4-8 watch, one AB is lookout on the bridge, one AB is at the wheel, an armed guard is forward, one armed guard is aft, an armed guard is on the starboard side of the bridge. Mr. Daly, the ship's purser, is keeping watch on the port station on the bridge, in place of a sick armed guardsman. Lt. Colwin is on the bridge, and I am standing by with the captain, keeping lookout.

At 7:30 p.m. the skipper sights a suspicious looking lump, or object, on the portside. He watches it closely and calls attention of the others to it. He is certain that it is a submarine. He tells Lt. Colwin to have the gun stations manned and ready for action. The captain calls the engine room for the best full speed possible, and explains why, to the chief engineer.

The submarine is holding our speed at about 12 knots, apparently assuming that she has not been seen, or just navigating into position for attack. Sparks, is notified to stand by for any emergency.

The captain orders a change of course. He hopes to leave the sub astern, possibly outrun her by running full speed.

At 7:50 p.m. a second sub is sighted ahead just slightly off the port bow. Another change of course is ordered, and we swing north. The second sub soon drops out of sight astern.

Lt. Colwin is attempting to sight the sub with his glasses and the 5 inch gun telescope, but is unable to make contact.

When the sub is well astern, the captain changes course back to westerly, executing the change by easy turns and 20 degree zigzag intervals, until we are on a course of 280. The entire crew, except for the black gang, is now on deck, keeping a sharp lookout.

At 8:19 p.m. the John Drayton is struck by a torpedo on the starboard side, directly in the engine room. A huge flame belched out of the stack. The ship shuddered. The engines stopped, and it became eerily quiet. No submarine is sighted.

The chief engineer rushes below and reports the engines are demolished, and a mass of steam is escaping. He believes engine cadet Jack Stadstad, oiler Clayton Spivey and a wiper, have been killed in the explosion. The master valve is closed. All lights, including emergency lights, are out.

There is no confusion on board. The crew, rapidly and silently, go to their assigned boat stations. Lifeboat #3, on the starboard side, was destroyed by the torpedo and has disappeared.

I walked quickly to my room, grab my Bowditch, my diary and a blanket and place them in my assigned lifeboat, #4.

While the lifeboat complement is still assembling, I rush back to the chart room and take the current chart and the chart case.

I got back to the #4 lifeboat, in a moment, but find the boat gone. It has disappeared in the darkness, with only a few men aboard.

The John Drayton, however, is not in immediate danger of sinking. Water in the engine room is at sea level and some water is entering #4 hold.

The crew is anxious to leave, expecting another torpedo or shell fire. Captain Norman orders "ABANDON SHIP!" and #1 and #2 lifeboats are lowered away.

The ship is heading northwest, making port the lee side, remarkably safe, despite the moderate southwesterly gale and high confused seas.

Crowded, #2 lifeboat on the port side is already in the water, getting ready to cast off. I scramble down the landing net, carrying the chart case and chart, when my foot gets caught in the net. Someone in the boat reaches up and frees my foot, and I tumble into #2 boat.

Some seamen are retching over the side. Two, covered with oil are sprawled on the bottom of the boat. Some men are fully dressed, others are shirtless. The smell of oil is sickening and overwhelming.

There is great anxiety to get away from the ship in expectation of another torpedo, enemy machine gun, or shell fire. The boat casts off, and we drift away from the ship. The weather is cold and the seas are high, but because of the oil slick, the waves are not breaking.

We see lifeboat #1 has capsized. The chief is on the overturned boat. We call softly to him to swim over, but he seems paralyzed and doesn't move, as the boat drifts away.

Sparks is on the stern of the ship signaling with a light. We call to him to jump, but he does not leave the ship. I thought for a moment, that his heavy brace would not allow him to stay afloat.

About 300 yards ahead, the conning tower of the submarine breaks the water and the submarine surfaces. We get down to the bottom of the lifeboat, expecting a burst of bullets, but there's no sound from the submarine.

Off in the distance, on the starboard side of the John Drayton, another submarine signals by blinker light and the two submarines exchange messages. We are well away from the ship, drifting closer to the first sub. We see the deck gun forward and then both subs open fire, shelling the John Drayton. I count 18 shots but the ship is still afloat.

We continue drifting away, keeping very quiet and low in the boat. The chief mate is at the tiller. The men in the boat are cold, wet, miserable and frightened, huddling together at the bottom of the boat for warmth and protection, afraid to show their heads over the gunwales in expectation of machine gun fire.

The wind and sea are increasing. The night becomes darker as heavy clouds obscure the moon. We are grateful for the darkness as we slip by the submarine.

At dawn, nothing is seen except ocean, no ship, no lifeboats, no rafts, no wreckage. We are alone, a strong gale is blowing, the chief mate estimates the seas at 40 feet and breaking over the gunwales. He is at the tiller looking ill and shivering with the cold and wet.

We count 24 men in the boat. Some had been assigned other boats, but crowded into #2 as the last chance to get away. There were the chief mate, Westover; the third mate, Pruitt; 3 cadets, Deitz, Kellegrew, and Rosen; 7 armed guard, including the coxswain, Travelstead and two signalmen; the bo'sun and 3 ABs, Tobiassen, Kardos, and Hudgins; ordinary seaman, Fontaine; plus oiler, Manley; fireman Woltjen; wiper, Brown and 4 messmen, including Chandler, Turner and Hutchinson.

Our last position on board the John Drayton on April 21, put us about 300 miles due east of Durban, South Africa. We did not know that Sparks had gotten a message off advising of our torpedoing, and after a short conference in the boat, we decided to sail for the coast, hoping, in the meantime, to be seen by a rescue plane or ship.

The seas were picking up. The gale became stronger with heavy, squally winds. Nick Tobiassen rigs the sea anchor and throws it over the stern to keep us running before the wind. Charlie Kardos is working the bilge pump and the seas are threatening to swamp the boat. Tobiassen shouts for everyone to lie on the bottom of the boat to keep us from capsizing.

Suddenly, the chief mate is gone, over the side, carrying with him a .38 caliber revolver, the only firearm aboard the boat. Tobiassen mans the tiller, while I keep an eye on the sea anchor. I feel Mr. Westover was sick, weak, and tired, and simply could not hold on any longer. The loss of the mate, further depresses the spirits in the boat. We had counted on his skill and seamanship to help us pull through.

The gale is still blowing and it is impossible to raise a sail. We hope to ride out the strong wind and rough sea and then sail for the coast. We will head northwest aware that the strong southeasterly Mozambique current will possibly make our course true west. We fear being swept too far south into the icy waters of the south Atlantic.

When the wind and the sea moderate somewhat, we check our gear and find a mast, sail, cans of pemmican, a cask of water with an enamel cup, flare gun and flares, bilge pump and a hatchet secured at the fore end of the boat.

After the loss of the chief mate, we turned to Mr. Pruitt, the 3rd mate, to take command, but he is ill, lying on the bottom of the boat, unable to take charge. In the meantime, Nick Tobiassen is handling the tiller and assuring everyone that we'll make it, even if we have to row. He is a natural, able leader and has the confidence of the men.

On the third day, the weather improves. A south African PBY

seems to be passing, without seeing the lifeboat, then it suddenly wheels and swoops over us, slowing and descending, as if to land. But the seas are too rough and the plane flies off. We are sure that we have been seen. Elated, and confident that we will soon be rescued, we open the water cask, joyfully, gulp large mouthfuls of water, and open cans of pemmican and pass them around. There is excitement and happiness in the boat, knowing that our ordeal will soon be over.

CHAPTER X

Capsized

The following day, the weather deteriorates. The winds change direction and increase. Breaking waves crash down upon us again. Planes fly overhead but move on. We have not been seen in the rough sea.

Messman Chandler begins raving and shouting, "I have to get out of here!" He stands up in the boat and then plunges over the side and is soon lost in the heavy sea.

The weather still does not permit us to rig the sail. There is intermittent calm but the wind soon picks up again and the sea becomes confused and treacherous.

The sea anchor keeps our stern to the waves but the constant pressure on it begins to fray the line. Nick is still at the tiller, tirelessly fighting to keep the boat afloat. Tommy Kellegrew, Mort Deitz and I relieve him from time to time.

Five days out, Turner, the messman, drops over the side and quickly disappears astern.

On the sixth day, we are seen again. The crew is elated. A PBY swoops low, and drops two packages into the waves. We are able to retrieve one, and the other disappears. On the package is written, 'DESTROYER LEAVING DURBAN.' Inside, we find eight 12 ounce cans of drinking water, malted milk tablets, chocolate, and chewing gum.

We wait hours, anxiously, peering at the horizon, but there is no sign of a destroyer. At night, we fire the flare gun, sending up 5 flares at 10 minute intervals but there is no response. Once again, spirits sink in despair. There is growing inertia and feeling of hopelessness.

At dawn, our 7th day in the boat, dark clouds are scutting across the sky. The winds pick up to gale force again, and stinging spray lashes the men. The seas become mountainous and constantly break into the boat. Charlie Kardos and Billy Fontaine work the bilge pump, but the boat is in danger of swamping. The men are cold, wet, and despairing, sitting in knee deep water. Nick has given up on trying to raise the sail. We cadets take turns at the tiller, and the sea anchor astern is on a tight leash, straining the line.

Suddenly, a rogue, mountainous, wave upends the boat, and all 21 of us are tossed into the sea. Some of us manage to cling to the overturned boat, but others start drifting away. Nick grabs the sea painter line, puts it between his teeth, swims to the men who are drifting away, and puts a loop around each man and gradually brings him back to the overturned boat.

Mr. Pruitt, climbs onto the overturned boat and in a frenzy starts screaming "SAVE US JESUS!" "JESUS, SAVE US!", "SAVE US, JESUS!" After a fierce struggle we finally pull the third mate off the boat.

Nick positions some men on either side of the boat, and after hours of desperate effort, another mountainous wave helps us to right it. Two of us scramble in and begin bailing with our hands and a bucket that had been secured to a thwart. We pull in one man at a time, who bails. Finally, a miracle! There are 21 men, all hands, back in the boat, but our loss is terrifying. The water, cans of food, sail, sea anchor, flare gun and flares, bilge pump, mirror, and chart are gone. I almost cried when I saw those cans of pemmican, bobbing on the sea and floating away, too far for any of us to reach. We have only oars, the chart case, bucket, drinking cup and hatchet.

All of us are exhausted. The weather is still bad and the seas are running high. Nick fashions another sea anchor from a flotation compartment under the lifeboat seat. He removes the compartment, punches holes in it with a pocket knife, and secures it with a sail halyard, and then throws it over the stern. It works! It slows the boat, keeping the wind and sea directly astern.

At dawn, morale is lifted when the sun breaks through and the weather begins to moderate. The navy signalman, who has been cutting notches on a thwart to mark the passage of days, reports 8 days in the boat.

The cold, the wet, the sea, lack of food, and exposure, are beginning to tell. Men are showing signs of deteriorating health. Feet are swollen, and skin is peeling from painful, and constant immersion in the sea water. Lips are parched and tempers are short.

Tommy Kellegrew, ever cheerful, says, "Let's row for it." He and Mort Deitz break out the oars. Nick and I pull in the sea anchor and we set our course northwest with the rising sun on the starboard quarter.

Hutchinson, the messman, takes up the bucket and begins bailing, gradually bringing down the water sloshing on bottom of the boat. Hunger and thirst are becoming unbearable now. We are constantly talking about ice water, hamburgers, ice cream, and cold beer.

Mr. Pruitt is babbling senselessly, and the old bo'sun is talking incessantly about going below for a cup of coffee.

Charlie Kardos and Billy Fontaine take turns at the oars. After awhile those of us who are able, spell them and I am surprised to find how heavy the oars are. I can barely manage to pull. The navy boys take their turn.

By mid day with the sun overhead, we are heading north and we feel we are making good time. In the afternoon, the sea is calm. Hutchinson is still bailing and the sun is now on our port quarter. Hours later, we are exhausted, heads down, panting for breath.

Some of the men have blisters and bleeding hands. At sunset, the sun is on our port bow and we desperately hope, with wind and current, we are on a northwest course. At night, we row the same course with the rising moon on the starboard quarter.

Some of us have lifejackets that carry dim little red lights for detection, when floating in the darkness. We take one of those lights and hang it on top of the mast, hoping that a passing ship may see it.

The night is cold, and we try to sleep at the bottom of the boat, huddling together for warmth. Some of the crew are nervous and jumpy, reaching time and again for cigarettes that aren't there. Wet shreds of tobacco and paper are floating on the bottom of the boat, which they scoop up, chew and swallow. At about midnight, exhausted, we quit rowing and rest on our oars. We are wet, cold and miserable.

April 29, my 24th birthday, dawned clear and bright. The boat is in the midst of a school of flying fish. Two fish land in the boat and I cut them into 21 pieces, one for each man. We swallow them over painful and swollen tongues.

Now the talk becomes obsessive about water. Some take the cup and drink a mixture of urine and salt water. Hallucinations begin and the young navy coxswain points ahead and says, "There's my wife," and walks over the side.

Mr. Pruitt is dead on the bottom of the boat and we put him over the side. Even Nick is discouraged, slumped over at the tiller.

Now one day runs into the next. The days are hot and the nights bitter cold. Men are half crazed and begin looking at each other suspiciously. Sharks are trailing the boat and one follows alongside daily, almost grazing the boat.

An albatross lands on the water about 10 feet away. I try to hit him with the oar, but he paddles away. He comes back again and again, and each time I try to hit him, he moves just out of reach.

It rains, occasionally, light rain, just enough to tease us. Hoping for a bit of fresh water, some men take to licking the thwarts, but they are salt encrusted.

I become half blind from looking out at the broiling sun and mirror-like sea.

Billy Fontaine collapses at the oars and is dead. Two navy gunners die. Another dies from drinking salt water, then another five in one day, and we lower them gently over the side.

Suddenly, Tommy Kellegrew takes off his clothes, climbs over the gunwale and starts to swim alongside. He beckons to us to join him, and Mort Deitz and I climb over. The water, momentarily, is strangely refreshing, but we are fearful of sharks, and soon turn back to the boat. My arms tremble with exertion, as I try to clamber back into the boat.

The days get hotter and the nights stay bitter cold. We strip off our clothes during the day, put them on again at night, huddling together, like animals, for warmth.

We are making very little headway now, simply drifting accompanied by the ever present sharks. Our bodies are wasted and it's difficult to sit with sores on our buttocks, faces and arms are blistered. Some men have bleeding hands and swollen and bleeding feet. Drinking salt water and urine is common. The men are acting crazy.

Nick Tobiassen, very weak, is lying on a thwart near me. His eyes wide open, he reaches over and whispers, "Take my sweater." At first I don't move, but he says again, "Take my sweater." Painfully, barely able, I remove the tight blue sweater.

Nick is dead soon afterwards. His blue eyes, the color of the sky, are wide open. Although for the past several days, Nick had been lethargic, barely moving and not speaking, we miss his leadership, his seamanship and the feeling of security he gave us. Somehow we felt Nick would find a way to save us.

A few of the men barely notice, but to others, the loss of Nick leaves us with little hope. Several of us struggle, and we gently put Nick over the side.

The bo'sun begins pushing and kicking the sleeping sailors, going wildly, from stem to stern, shouting, again and again, "I'm going below for coffee!" Screaming, Travelstead grabs the hatchet and hits him a tremendous blow on the head, cracking his skull. The bo'sun falls to the bottom of the boat. He's dead lying face up.

Travelstead takes the hatchet, and opens the bo'sun's chest, cleaving him up the center. Then he takes the cup from Hutchinson and dips it in the pool of blood in the bo'sun's abdomen, and drinks it.

The crazed sailors, like in a primitive ritual, solemnly line up, dip and drink, passing the cup from man to man. Not everyone in the boat participates. The bo'sun's body is put over the side. The cup is handed back to Hutchinson who begins bailing again. No one mentions the incident again.

The following morning, 22 days in the boat, heavy clouds gather in the southwest accompanied by thunder and lightning. In the afternoon, we are hit by a tremendous rainstorm.

Joyously, with rain in our faces, we take off all our clothes, stretch them out over the thwarts, and sit naked in the boat, while our bodies soak up the rain. The bucket in the bottom of the boat is collecting rainwater. We wring out our clothes, again and again, over the bucket. When the rain is over, the bucket is more than half full. By nightfall, we are not so parched, and we sleep, knowing that there is a small supply of water for several days.

At dawn, Travelstead is dead. His stomach is distended from drinking our rainwater. The bucket is overturned, and our precious water, mixed now with sea water, is sloshing in the bottom of the boat.

Days pass, and the men do not move now. Mort Deitz is intoning Hebrew prayers. Tom Kellegrew is stretched out on the seat, his head hanging low. Two navy men are forward. Bill Manley and Alfred Woltjen are slumped over on the boat's curved seat. Robert Browning, formerly heavy, but now just skin and bones is on the bottom of the boat. I am at the stern, my eyes heavily encrusted, swollen, and burning.

The only sound is made by Hutchinson who bails, scraping the drinking cup on the bottom of the boat. No hand is on the tiller, and the boat rolls gently in the troughs. I place Tommy's head on my knee.

The following morning, even Hutchinson is quiet. The bailing cup is on the seat next to his body.

Later, we hear the sound of a motor. It gets louder as it approaches, and we see almost overhead, a PBY Catalina flying boat. We raise our arms and try to wave, expecting the plane like the others, to pass over, but it circles, again and again. The pilot waves to us, and flies off.

There is restrained joy in our boat. We think, will he return, will they find us? Hours pass, and we are convinced it is another cruel hoax.

Deep gloom settles in the boat. Tommy is dead. I carefully put his head down on the seat. Hutchinson and Woltjen are not stirring.

Suddenly, there is a rasping shout from the navy signalman. He sees a ship approaching, and he stands, braced against the mast, and waves. My heart begins to race and pound, uncontrollably. I try to slow it, by turning away, but it doesn't help. It races and I feel faint.

Soon, the SS Mount Rhodope, a Greek vessel, is alongside and sailors gently carry us up to the deck, where we are stretched out against the wheelhouse. They massage our wrists with alcohol and prepare chicken broth and hot tea with condensed milk which we sip slowly. They secure our lifeboat astern.

CHAPTER XI

Addington Military Hospital

In a few hours we are in Durban. Ambulances are at the dock, and we are taken to Addington Military Hospital. The captain of the Rhodope has given each of us a card, printed with the Greek, American and British flags, and underneath he wrote, "SS Mount Rhodope, Greke, save us." He is a brave man with a brave crew. They saved our lives.

On arrival at the hospital, my racing heart begins to slow down. Three of us, Mort Deitz, Bill Manley and I, are brought into a ward of wounded and recovering British servicemen. The two navy men in our boat are taken to a navy hospital.

Our shipmates, Herman Hutchinson, messman; Robert Browning, wiper; Alfred Woltjen, fireman; and my buddy, Cadet midshipman, Thomas Kellegrew are dead. They were buried in the Stellawood Cemetery, Durban North, Natal, South Africa, a long way from home.

When picking us up, the captain of the Rhodope said our position was southeast of Durban, about 40 miles offshore. Fortunately for us, we were in a shipping lane. We had traveled about 250 miles by rowing, aided by wind and a southeasterly sea. We had made an average of about 8 miles a day. The Mozambique channel current had swept us slightly south of our target.

We had spent 30 days in the lifeboat. We started out with a complement of 24 men, 19 of whom died. Left were the 5 survivors, one aged 18, two at 22, one at 24 and one 25 years old.

Examined in the hospital, I weighed 97 pounds, down from 140. I was listed as suffering from exposure, malnutrition, dehydration, emaciation, septic abrasions of the hands and feet, conjunctivitis of both eyes, and shock. Mort Deitz and Bill Manley were in similar condition. Mort, also suffered painful immersion of the feet, and his hospital bed was fitted with a small bamboo cage to protect his feet from the pressure of sheets and blanket.

On the second day in the hospital, I had a surprising visitor. I could barely see him through half blind, salt encrusted eyes.

He introduced himself, "My name is Jock. I'm the pilot who spotted your lifeboat." Jock was a slim, little guy, "who came to see how the Yanks were doing."

I thanked him and told him he saved our lives.

He said a number of Allied ships had been torpedoed off the coast of South Africa by German and Italian submarines.

"In your case," Jock said, "recent heavy storms and strong gales made it unlikely that a lifeboat would survive."

"Orders were received weeks ago," he said, "to search for you, and we did search. But hope was given up after many days of heavy weather."

Jock said, "It was only, by chance, on routine patrol that I saw you."

He stayed for a few minutes. On leaving, Jock shook my hand and impulsively took off his flight jacket, laid it on my bed and smiled, "Yank, keep this as a war souvenir from South Africa. Good luck and stay out of lifeboats."

Several days later, a South African army officer was ushered to my bedside by Head Sister Margaret Fraser, who introduced Captain Stein, army doctor and psychiatrist.

Captain Stein shook my hand and as the nurse left, said he had been told of our ordeal and wondered if I wanted to talk about it.

I told him, "No thanks. I just want to get stronger, gain some weight and get home."

He said, "I understand and if at any time you change your mind, I can be reached through Sister Fraser."

The care and attention we received at the hospital were outstanding, and we recovered quickly. A newspaper article of our rescue appeared in the Natal Daily News, and the Durban community was generous with invitations.

We were anxious, however, to get home. Bill Manley left on a ship to the States after four weeks, and after five weeks in hospital, Mort Deitz and I returned to New York on the C-3 army transport, General George W. Goethels.

Deitz and I separated in New York. I was sent to the Merchant Marine hospital in Stapleton, Staten Island for stomach distress, where I was put on a Sippy diet for several days.

While at the hospital, I called the Hutchinson and Kellegrew families. I could not reach the Stadstads.

I told the Hutchinsons how conscientious and brave their husband and father was, how he bailed, literally, day and night, how he died at his post, and how we found him at the end, with his bailing cup nearby. He had bailed with his last strength, keeping the boat dry, and saving us from swamping. He was steady and steadfast, a real hero. The Hutchinsons, who lived in Harlem, New York, were very grateful.

Mrs. Kellegrew, Tom's mother, insisted on coming to Stapleton, Staten Island to see me. We arranged a date for the following day, and I met her in the hospital courtyard.

Immediately, I saw the resemblance of Tommy and his mother. We sat on a bench and I told her what great friends Tom and I were. She nodded and took out of her purse the picture that Tommy and I had taken in Iran, when he was seated on a chair in mid-street, and I was standing beside him.

Tom had written home many times telling of our adventures

ashore and our activities aboard ship. I told her what an outstanding engineer Tom was and how the chief praised him, how Tom planned to make a career of the sea, and how much he enjoyed life aboard ship.

I told Mrs. Kellegrew that Tom's constant good humor and leadership kept up morale in the lifeboat and finally, how he rowed day after day, taking the turns of others.

Mrs. Kellegrew took out of her purse a pocketwatch, engraved TK, Tom's initials, and insisted that I take it. She said Tom would have wanted me to have it. I thanked her for the watch and told her I would treasure it.

We cried over Tommy. He was 20 years old. When we parted, she kissed me, goodbye.

Three days later, after a hospital diet of only milk and cream, I was offered a medical discharge, based on a probable ulcer and my ordeal in the lifeboat. I weighed 118 pounds, still experiencing some stomach pain.

I told the doctor, if possible, I would prefer to stay in the service. I pointed out, I was due to report to the academy for nine months ashore, where, with the proper diet and medical supervision, I expected my health to improve. He thought about it for a moment and he agreed. He ordered one month medical leave at home.

For the first time since arrival in the States, I called home and told them, I would be there shortly. I hadn't called earlier, because I didn't want to mention the hospital, or my condition. I had cabled and written them from South Africa and I knew they were aware I was safe.

There was great joy in the household when I arrived. My parents had received two telegrams, one from the Coast Guard, followed by another from the War Shipping Administration.

The Coast Guard wire informed my parents, YOUR SON, HERMAN ROSEN IS MISSING AND PRESUMED LOST FOLLOWING ACTION IN THE PERFORMANCE OF HIS DUTY AND IN THE SERVICE OF HIS COUNTRY.

I could only imagine the shock, the despair and the tears in my house on receipt of that wire.

Later that night, another wire was delivered from the War Shipping Administration, informing my parents IT WAS FIRST THOUGHT YOUR SON HERMAN ROSEN WAS AMONG THE MISSING MEN OF HIS VESSEL DESTROYED BY ENEMY ACTION. FURTHER INFORMATION SHOWS HE SURVIVED. WE ARE GLAD PREVIOUS INFORMATION SENT IS NOT TRUE.

Apparently the Navy waited 30 days before advising that missing seamen are presumed lost. We were found on the 30th day. The two telegrams were sent and received on the same day. Of course, there was great joy and relief in the household. It was felt, it was truly a miracle.

Several days later my folks received another telegram. This time from Addington Military Hospital in Durban, South Africa.

NURSE FRASER ADDINGTON HOSPITAL DURBAN ASKS WE SEND WORD YOUR SON SAFE AND WELL THERE WRITING. SIGNED, SISTER MARGARET FRASER.

I spent almost six weeks at home, eating, sleeping, and generally recovering. Captain Norman called with good wishes. He had been in touch with my family, several times since the end of May, when he learned we were rescued. He wanted to get together and hear about our lifeboat experience, but he had been shipping out and was leaving again soon. He promised to call on his return.

I was ordered to report back to the academy for further training on September 9, 1943. I was now a first classman, nine months to graduation.

Our course of study included, nautical science, gunnery, navigation, marine cargo operations, seamanship, naval architecture, marine electronics, astronomy, meteorology, oceanography, marine collision prevention, science, English, mathematics, and Rules of the Road.

During this period, I was managing editor of Polaris, the academy magazine and I was inducted into the "Tin Fish" club, whose membership was made up of cadet/midshipmen, who were torpedoed or forced to abandon ship due to enemy action.

The medical officer had given me a pass and at 2200, lights

out, I was permitted to go to the galley for milk, cake or cookies, added calories to help me put on some weight.

After nine months of study and successfully passing final exams, in order to graduate, we had to pass a license examination given by the Coast Guard "to certify our proficiency in the operation of the deck or engine department of an American merchant vessel."

One day at the academy, I was called to the office of the Commandant of Cadets and told to report to naval intelligence, downtown New York, the following Saturday at 10:00 a.m.

I duly reported and was ushered into a room, where a navy commander produced my John Drayton diary, somewhat torn, covers gone, bearing signs of sea immersion. He told me it was in #4 lifeboat with 11 survivors, when they were picked up by the Swedish MV Oscar Gorthon at 0900 GCT on April 23, and landed at Lourenco Marques, Portugese East Africa on April 25, 1943.

The commander looked stern and said some of the information in the log could be considered secret. Then he smiled, gave me the diary and said, "I bet you thought you'd never see it again."

CHAPTER XII

Captain Carl Norman

I was graduated on June 6, 1944. We were awarded Bachelor of Science degrees, licenses as 3rd mate or 3rd assistant engineer in the Merchant Marine and commissioned as Ensign in the U.S. Naval Reserve.

My parents and Captain Norman were present at graduation. The captain presented me with a gift, which, unbelievably, was my camera he had appropriated in New York in September, 1942. I had been taking unauthorized pictures on deck, while the John Drayton was loading cargo. Captain Norman, at that time, promised to take care of the camera and return it to me. I told him how grateful I was to get the camera and how meaningful it was to me.

The captain was anxious to hear about our lifeboat, but I pressed him to tell us about how he survived the torpedoing and managed to save the camera.

We adjourned to the academy canteen and over coffee, he said, there were two, possibly three submarines in the attack. He thought they were Japanese judging from the dolphin shape of the conning tower.

His assigned lifeboat, #3 was destroyed by the torpedo, and after #2 and #4 were launched safely, he gave permission to make ready to lower #1. The second mate, Mr. Kemp, was at the falls. Chief Brainovich, AB Soderberg, oiler Rae and one armed guard were in the boat.

Then the captain went to the radio shack to make sure Sparks had transmitted our SOS. He and Sparks went to join lifeboat #1 and found the boat, already in the water, swung away from the ship's side.

Mr. Kemp and several crew members, using the boat's painter were unable to bring the boat back alongside. The seas were rough and the boat capsized, spilling the chief, Soderberg, Rae and the navy gunner into the sea.

The captain then ordered the rafts and doughnut floats released, and the men in the water and those still on board were advised to make for the rafts. At the same time, enemy shell fire began.

As a raft was drifting by, the captain jumped, swam a few strokes and made the raft. He was covered with oil. They called to Sparks to jump, but he didn't leave the ship. The captain said he had hoped that Sparks and the four men in the overturned boat got to one of the rafts.

There were 14 men on his raft, including Mr. Kemp, who had saved the captain's briefcase, Mr. Daly, purser, Lt. Colwin, a number of armed guard, and two messmen. He said they saw the sub and expected machine gun fire.

We were amazed at the captain's ability to recall the details, but he said the picture was very vivid in his mind. During the first night on the raft, he said, the wind increased to gale force and the seas about 40 feet high tossed the raft at times, near beam's end.

The next morning, the gale winds continued. Nothing could be seen of the ship or lifeboats. One raft, about a half mile away was empty. Hatch boards were floating around, evidently the ship was sunk and the hatch boards broke loose. No one on the raft was injured and there was no apparent hunger or thirst. The wind continued from the southeast and the captain felt that the raft was setting toward the coast, about 300 miles away, at 1-1/2 to 2 miles per hour. They served the first lunch, two biscuits, one package of malted milk tablets, and two ounces of water per person.

The following day, the weather was the same. The winds were southerly, the food was rationed, the same amount, two ounces of water, biscuits, malted milk tablets, and a little pemmican.

The captain said his personal log, some letters and my camera were in the briefcase the second mate had brought aboard and that he continued to make entries in the log. He tried to keep everyone cheerful saying they would surely make land at the rate the raft was setting west, but he feared a change in wind or sea could easily set them south, where they would be lost, far from the shipping lanes.

That day, he said, they saw sharks nearby. There were only a few complaints on board and morale was generally good. Strangely, the captain said the raft appeared to grow smaller each day.

On the sixth day on the raft, the weather was warmer. The men were thirsty, still only getting two ounces per day.

They, suddenly, sighted a Catalina flying boat zigzagging, apparently searching. They were sighted. The plane, heading directly toward them, dropped 3 flares and signalled HELP IS NEAR. The plane dropped smoke signals and soon a destroyer was seen. The captain broke out the rations and the men had 8 ounces of water.

The destroyer, HMS Relentless, arrived, brought the survivors aboard and destroyed the raft by shell fire. They were picked up 160 miles southeast of Durban and they were in Durban the following morning.

Lt. Colwin and the armed guard, went to a navy installation, the captain and the merchant crew were taken to the Seaman's Institute. He checked with the Navy about #2 and #4 lifeboats, but there was no news to report.

Days later, he said he was feeling okay, but still stiff and suffering from bruises and salt water sores. He inquired, again and again of the American Consul and the navy about the two missing lifeboats. One day, he was told that one boat with about 20 men was sighted, and he had the feeling that the two boats would be safe. He stayed around the Navy office the following day, but there was no further news of the boats.

On Monday, May 3, the captain was told that our boat was sighted by the destroyer, Relentless, but because of mountainous seas, the Relentless was unable to pick up survivors.

The captain's health had gradually improved and he was told to be ready to leave Durban, at short notice, with the merchant marine crew. He said, goodbye, to Lt. Colwin and the navy armed guard, still hoping lifeboats #2 and #4 had landed safely on some isolated part of the coast.

The following day, he boarded the SS Robin Tuxford with Kemp, Daly, and two messmen, Prior and McGrew, bound for home. They stopped in East New London, South Africa, for loading provisions, cargo, and fuel.

The captain went ashore to inquire again about the lifeboats and he was told one arrived in Durban in tow of a Coast Guard vessel. It was good news, but the next day it was reported that the lifeboat was from an English vessel. There was no further news of #2 and #4. They left New London for Capetown, and Prior, who became ill on board, was left in the hospital in Capetown.

After Capetown, the skipper said they stopped in Bahia, Brazil for fuel and water and finally arrived in New York on June 4 when he learned that lifeboats #2 and #4 had been picked up, #4 with 11 survivors, and #2 with five.

The captain said the original complement of the John Drayton was 56 men, 41 merchant marine and 15 armed guard. He had been told 21 merchant marine crew and five navy armed guard were lost as a result of the torpedoing.

It was getting late and the skipper had to leave. He was spending a short time ashore with his wife, Betty. He was looking forward to sailing with me, now that I had my new 3rd mate's license. We hoped to work it out.

In June, 1944, the war in Europe had turned in favor of the allies. Despite huge losses, troops had landed on the beach at Normandy. In Italy, hundreds of Sherman tanks and thousands of allied troops fought their way north from the beach at Anzio. Merchant vessels in the front lines were pouring men and supplies into the battle.

CHAPTER XIII

Back at Sea

One week after graduation, I signed on the SS Helen as 3rd mate with Captain J.A. Abram. We ran alone to the Carribbean despite submarine activity, and we brought back to the States tons of sugar for the armed forces and domestic consumption.

After the trip, it was felt I had enough sea time and experience to sit for my 2nd mate's license. I studied and passed the exam in a week and signed on the Helen again with Captain Abram in my new capacity as second mate.

Again, we went to the Caribbean running alone, with supplies for army and navy installations in Puerto Rico and the Virgin Islands. We returned to the states with general cargo.

I signed off August 28. Captain Abram was disappointed. He said I was doing a great job as navigating officer and hoped I would continue to sail with him on the Helen. However, I wanted to sail foreign instead of coastwise, and see the war in Europe first hand.

Fortunately, there was a second mate's berth open on the SS Marina, a sleek new ship built in 1941 commanded by Captain

Charles Hendrick. I signed on the Marina as second mate, August 30, 1944, two days after leaving the Helen.

U.S. and British troops were invading the south of France, near Cannes, and on August 25, German troops in Paris surrendered. There was a feeling in the States that the end of the war in Europe was in sight, although it would be almost a year before all German forces unconditionally surrendered.

The Marina was loaded with ammunition, jeeps, essential war supplies, and airplanes in crates. We also carried about 50 U.S. Air Force pilots. Our port of destination was Cherbourg, France, recently liberated by allied forces.

We sailed in convoy, about 22 ships of various nationalities. There were no lumbering Liberty ships or coal burners in the convoy. We averaged about 15 knots, under the watchful eyes of two destroyers and two corvettes.

Coming off watch at 4:00 a.m. one morning, I witnessed the largest crap game I have ever seen. The pilots, it seemed like all 50 of them, were in the officers' mess. Thousands of dollars were on the deck, and the dice were rolling against the bulkhead.

It was well into the war now and apparently the navy was learning to deal with the submarine threat. Although 9 ships were sunk in July, and 4 in August, the Merchant Marine was no longer experiencing the huge losses of men and ships as in 1942 and 1943, when the monthly toll often exceeded 40 or 50 ships and hundreds of merchant seamen.

Our trip to Cherbourg was uneventful, despite the usual alerts and alarms. While the Marina was discharging cargo, I got a lift in a jeep with two army officers who were heading to their base, a short distance from town. We saw chalked in bold letters around Cherbourg, "VIVE LE MAQUIS," an unforgettable sight for me, and truly a testament to the French resistance who were stubbornly fighting the Germans.

We returned to New York October 30, 1944. I stayed on the Marina with Captain Hendrick, as second mate. We loaded cargo, food and war materiel, and sailed in convoy, again, for the United Kingdom on November 9.

Keeping watch on the bridge in the North Atlantic in winter is a misery. Freezing rain and cold winds coat the rigging with sheets of ice. The deck becomes a slick hazard as the ship pitches and rolls in the rough seas.

Station keeping was nearly impossible. Ships, battered by sea and wind, lost positions and it was a constant matter of calling the engine room for a change in revolutions, or ordering the helmsmen to go "right a bit," or "easy left." Ships were blacked out and on moonless nights, a neighboring ship would suddenly loom up, so close, as to almost touch.

Navigation was haphazard. Only occasionally, did I get a sun sight or a star fix. We depended mainly on dead reckoning trying to estimate wind and sea drift. The convoy escorts darted back and forth like shepherd dogs after straying sheep. Occasional depth charges went off adding to the tension. The prospect of abandoning ship and being in the icy waters of the Atlantic was not a happy one.

We made the U.K. port of Swansea, Wales, where we delivered part of our cargo to allied troops.

One blacked out night, several of us visited a local pub and heard an impromptu performance of Welsh songs by the standup customers at the bar. The voices were excellent and the beer was warm, but our welcome was neither excellent, nor warm. The Welshmen were angry at the Yanks. They complained loudly, spoiling for a fight, that our troops were "overpaid, oversexed and over here."

The Welsh countryside was bleak, cold, dark, and wet. Huge slag hills were dumped around town and the people seemed to reflect their surroundings.

Our next port in the U.K. was Bournemouth, England, directly across the channel from Cherbourg, France, where we unloaded the balance of our cargo, food, jeeps, and munitions into the willing hands of American troops. After 3 days in port, we headed home.

The Marina's captain, Charles Hendrick was a short, muscular man, jumpy and withdrawn, a tightly wound spring of nervous energy. On my watch, he paced the bridge, hands deep in his heavy woolen coat and his head low in his collar. His constant appearance on the bridge made me wonder if he didn't trust my judgment, or simply, wanted to talk. I tried conversation, but he was uncommunicative. With him close by, my watch seemed cold and long. I was glad to be relieved at 4:00 a.m.

We returned to New York at the end of December, 1944. Sharp lookouts were posted on all sides of the ship. The Navy gun crew was on constant alert. The war at sea had picked up. Sixteen merchant ships were sunk or damaged during the month.

I was not feeling well, experiencing intermittent stomach pain. I took leave at home for two weeks, and feeling better, signed on the SS Babcock, a Liberty ship, as second mate, with Captain I.P. Thompson.

While on sick leave at home, news broke about a new German offensive in the Ardennes. Details were grim. The American army was trapped, caught completely unprepared, casualties were high, weather biting cold and men suffering frostbite, lack of munitions, food, and supplies. It was the Nazi last effort to beat back the allied advance, the Battle of the Bulge.

The Babcock loaded general cargo of food, jeeps, truck parts, and munitions and sailed for the Mediterranean in a convoy of 30 ships.

For several days we had overhead protection of observation balloons, in addition to the usual destroyers, sub chasers, and corvettes. We passed watchful eyes at Gibraltar and entered the Mediterranean the end of March, tying up in Marseilles, early April.

Efficient U.S. black troops, schooled in handling cargo, began unloading. On April 12, while in port, the radio operator rushed to the captain with an urgent message. It was addressed to the Armed Forces and ships at sea. "The President of the United States, Franklin D. Roosevelt, is dead."

We informed the black soldiers who were working the cargo. They stopped work and many sat down and cried, tears rolling down their faces. All of us, merchant marine crew, naval armed guard, and stevedore troops felt we had lost our leader, and we feared a setback in the war effort.

Captain Thompson of the Babcock was the complete opposite of Hendrick of the Marina. Thompson was young, about 38, relaxed and friendly, interested in his officers and crew. The Babcock was a happy ship. The mates ran their watches and the captain was not "tweaking the lines."

We left France mid April, 1945. I was suffering stomach pain again and anxious to get back to the States to get medical attention. Captain Thompson was supportive. He ordered the steward department to prepare a special diet for me with lots of milk, and eggs, and no spicy food. We traveled home, in convoy for the most part, zigzagging when running alone.

In April, German subs were still active in the Med and the north Atlantic. Fifteen U.S. ships were sunk or damaged during the month.

At sea, on May 7 we learned that General Jodl, chief of staff, surrendered all German armies and the war in Europe was over.

The Babcock arrived New York the following day, May 8, 1945 to a scene of wild celebration. Captain Thompson urged me to sign on again for a quick trip to England with food and supplies, and to bring American troops home. He promised a special diet again. I thanked him, but I left the Babcock for the Marine Hospital on Staten Island. The following day, May 9, 1945, I received an Honorable Discharge from the Merchant Marine.

At home, I called Captain Norman, who was planning a few more trips before retiring. He told me that the Marina, the ship I sailed on as second mate, struck a mine near Le Havre and was badly damaged. There were no casualties, but the ship was beached near Le Havre. However, he was puzzled and saddened, his friend, Captain Hendrick had died soon afterwards.

Several days later, the War Shipping Administration called and offered me a job recruiting men for the merchant marine. Anyone with a license, or any sea experience, was desperately needed for the huge sealift needed to bring home the army from Europe, and to transport soldiers and war materiel to the Pacific for the final stages of the war against Japan.

I joined the WSA and traveled Western Pennsylvania and Ohio, speaking at Union halls and town meetings, for several months, with limited success. In July, I met the lovely Susan, and we were married the following year.

CHAPTER XIV

War's End

The atom bomb was dropped August 6, 1945, and Japan surrendered, September 2, 1945, ending World War II.

During the following years, Captain Norman and I kept in touch through letters and an occasional phone call. His wife, Betty, died and he retired from the sea. The captain later, married Maria and bought a house with 28 acres in, of all places, Neversink, New York, in the Catskill mountains.

He and Maria invited Sue and me and our three children to visit in Neversink. When we arrived, he bounded out of the house in warm welcome, but I could see the children were disappointed. I took him aside and asked that he put on his uniform.

In a few minutes he came down, resplendent in dress blues, "scrambled eggs" hat, and four stripes. The kids were happy. Then he suggested that we all go berry picking. It was an unforgettable sight, the captain in his blue uniform, four stripes, hat, shirt, and tie, picking berries in the woods.

In the evening, he and I walked alone. He said, "I have 28 acres, I'll give you 14 if you build a house nearby." I was touched and thanked him, but said, I couldn't support a family living in Neversink. Nevertheless, I was deeply gratified.

Some years later he sent me his personal log of the trip of the John Drayton. Describing the log, he wrote, "Just writing about what happened, day to day, from October 10, 1942 to Wednesday, April 21, 1943, the day you'll never forget. Don't return the log to me, it's yours to keep. If there is anything more you would like to know, please ask me. At the same time, if we meet again, I may also wish to ask you some things. Keep well, love to you all, signed, Carl."

Captain Norman died in January, 1978. He was cleaning snow from his roof in Neversink. He fell and struck his head.

One year later, Maria sent me the captain's stopwatch he had used for navigation, and my picture that, "he would not part with." I felt the loss of the captain, deeply. He was more than my friend and mentor. I felt, I had lost my second father.

Later that year, as Associate National Director of the United Jewish Appeal, I attended a conference on philanthropy and charitable giving, in Philadelphia. While walking through the hotel corridor to a meeting, a tall, gentleman, tapped me on the shoulder. "Hank Rosen," he said, "I'm Morton Deitz."

We hugged, we hadn't seen each other in 35 years. We arranged to have dinner with our wives that evening, and reminisced about the John Drayton and our shipmates. Mort had gone to law school and became a tax attorney. It was good seeing him, and noting that the world had treated him well.

A couple of years ago, I received a phone call from Robert Morris, from Meridian, Mississippi. He had gotten my number from Kings Point. Morris, and his dear friend Billy Fontaine, were ordinary seamen aboard the John Drayton. Morris had been in lifeboat #4 with ten others. 17 men had been assigned to #4, including Billy Fontaine and me.

Morris wanted to know how his pal, Billy died. I told him, Billy was courageous in the lifeboat. He was cheerful and optimistic and did more than his share of rowing. In fact, his heart gave out, while he was pulling an oar.

I told Morris, we had great respect for Billy and we were proud to call him a shipmate. Morris thanked me, and said, he would give that information to Billy's family.

Morris said, while abandoning ship, a messman had prematurely let go of lifeboat #4, and the boat drifted toward the surfaced submarine. He heard the sub's engine, then the sub was alongside and a heaving line was thrown into the lifeboat. A man on deck with a machine gun, ordered in English, "One man, come on board."

The crew in the lifeboat pleaded with Morris to go, and with the aid of a big wave, he leaped into the hands of four, he thought at first, were German sailors.

An officer questioned him in English, asking the name of the ship, cargo, where bound, where they had been, where the torpedo hit. All the answers seemed to go well, except when Morris said, the ship was empty. The captain seemed displeased with the answer, and abruptly turned around and said, "goodbye."

Morris, certain now that the sub was Italian, was relieved to get back into the lifeboat unharmed, as the sub moved away.

He said, on the second day in the boat they saw a single engine plane, but were not spotted. On the third day, they were picked up by a Swedish vessel and taken to Laurenco Marques, Portugese East Africa, where he inquired about lifeboat #2. There was no news.

The survivors were in Laurenco Marques, a neutral port, for about one month before getting passage back to the States.

Morris said, to this day, he often thinks of Billy Fontaine, and knows he would have been saved, if he was able to get into lifeboat #4.

On August 25, 1998, I received a letter from Yuli M. Vorontsov, Ambassador of the Russian Federation to the United States. "Dear Sir, on behalf of President Boris Yeltzin, the Russian Government, and the entire Russian people, I am pleased to inform you that you have been awarded the Commemorative Medal, the 50th Anniversary of the Victory in the Great Patriotic War, WWII.

"This Medal is awarded to you in recognition of your courage and personal contribution to the Allied support of Russia during her fight for freedom against Nazi Germany.

"Please accept my heartfelt congratulations and wishes for your good health, well being, and every success."

Sincerely, Yuli M. Vorontsov.

"Enclosed is the commemorative medal and medal certificate."

I appreciated the medal and remembered our time in Iran, and the delivery of planes, tanks and munitions to the Russians.

It was good knowing the John Drayton and her crew had played a part in the victory over Nazi Germany. In fact, I learned that Chief Mate Oliver Westover and 3rd Assistant Engineer Vernon Hood were honored by having Liberty ships named after them.

Last year, the SS Lane Victory, a ship closely resembling a Liberty, visited the port of San Diego. Its crew were all volunteers, former WW II merchant seamen and naval armed guard.

My wife Sue, and I visited the ship. I showed her my room, the wheelhouse, the engine room. Then she said, "Show me your lifeboat."

We walked to #4 and then to #2. The boat looked so small and fragile.

I thought of the 30 days and 30 nights, of the mountainous seas; the 24 men shivering and huddled together for warmth; of the morning we put five of our shipmates over the side; the sounds of Hutchinson bailing, scraping the bottom of the boat with the tin cup; the raving madness and the pitiful moans for water; the loud crack on the head when the crazed Travelstead killed the bo'sun; and, of my two friends and fellow cadets, Tom Kellegrew and Jack Stadstad, so young, so courageous . . .

An old man now, I held Sue's hand, and we both cried.

#

To the best of my recollection, the foregoing account is true. Some of the events described, however, occurred sixty or more years ago, and recollections do dim in time. There may be some errors, therefore, of time and place.

For these, I apologize.

Herman Rosen
San Diego, California
June, 2002

PICTURES

Cadet/Midshipman Jack Stadstad

Cadet/Midshipman Thomas Kellegrew

Cadet/Midshipman Herman E. Rosen

C/M Herman Rosen in Addington Military Hospital,
Durban, South Africa, soon after rescue

NBJ356 20 COLLECT =53 CT3 3 EXTRA=RUTHERGLENGLASGOW 19

1943 JUL 24 PM 11 33

JOIN ROSEN=

1330 BEACH 41 ST EDGEMERE LI NY=

NURSE FRASER ADDINGTON HOSPITAL DURBAN ASKS US SEND WORD

YOUR SON SAFE AND WELL THERE WRITING=

=MARGARET FRASER.

Telegram from Head Sister Fraser,
Addington Military Hospital to Rosen Family

A Week on a Raft

Captain Carl Norman

S/S John Drayton survivors, fully recovered, Addington Military Hospital. Top row, 2nd left, Bill Manley; 3rd left, Morton Deitz; seated, bottom row, far right Herman Rosen. Seated center, Head Sister Margaret Fraser. Others are British servicemen.

# EPILOGUE (A)

The Italian submarine, the Leonardo da Vinci, which torpedoed the S/S John Drayton, April 21, 1943, was sunk by HMS Ness and HMS Active off the Azores, on May 23, 1943.

 # EPILOGUE (B)

In providing the lifeline from the U.S. to allied forces during the war, the American Merchant Marine suffered heavy losses in ships and men. More than 700 ships and close to 7,000 merchant marine seamen, all volunteers, were killed. The Merchant Marine, sustained a higher proportion of casualties, than all branches of the armed forces, with the exception of the Marine Corps.

210 Kings Point cadets and graduates were killed in action. The U.S. Merchant Marine Academy is the only federal academy permitted to carry a battle flag, indicating that its cadets, as students, were actively engaged in facing the enemy.

At the end of the war, Dwight D. Eisenhower, General of the Army said, "When final victory is ours, there is no service that will share its credit more deservedly than the Merchant Marine."

Chester W. Nimitz, Admiral of the Fleet said, "Not one of us who fought in the late war can forget, nor should any citizen be allowed to forget, that the national resources, which enabled us to carry the war to the enemy, and fight in his territory, and not our own, was carried in the ships of our merchant marine. They maintained the services of transport and supply."

 # EPILOGUE (C)

In 1988, 43 years after World War II, Congress belatedly conferred Veteran status on seamen who had served aboard U.S. Merchant Vessels during the war.

ABOUT THE AUTHOR

Herman "Hank" Rosen graduated from the U.S. Merchant Marine Academy and served as a ship's officer during WWII in the Atlantic, Pacific, Mediterranean, and Middle East. He was awarded the Combat Ribbon with Star, the Merchant Marine Mariner's Medal and the Victory Medal of the Great Patriotic War, by the Russian Government.

After the war, he earned a Master's Degree from New York University and enjoyed a successful career in public relations and fundraising.

He lives in San Diego with his wife Susan. They have three children and two grandchildren.

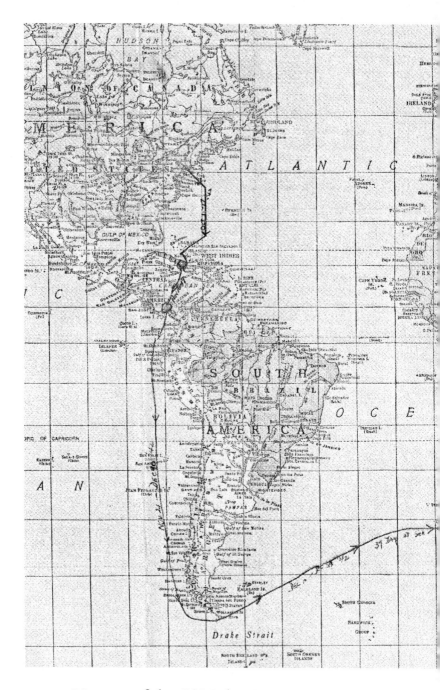

Voyage of the S/S John Drayton

Jan. 26 1943

TORPEDOED
APRIL 21, 1943

Printed in the United States
22114LVS00001B/138